£13.95

Richard Wentworth's

# Thinking Aloud

Ware Centre

Scotts

With an essay by Nick Groom

National Touring Exhibitions

Published on the occasion of *Thinking Aloud*, a National Touring Exhibition organised by the Hayward Gallery, London for the Arts Council of England.

Exhibition curated by Richard Wentworth

Exhibition tour:
Kettle's Yard, Cambridge
7 November 1998 – 3 January 1999
Cornerhouse, Manchester
9 January – 28 February
Camden Arts Centre, London
9 April – 30 May

Exhibition organised by Roger Malbert, assisted by Miranda Stacey, Julia Risness and Jessica White

Catalogue designed by Herman Lelie
Typeset by Stefania Bonelli
Printed in England by PJ Print Group

Front cover: *Hazard warning sign*. Photo: Mike Parsons
Back cover: *Endroit fréquenté par des enfants* (French street sign). Photo: Mike Parsons

Published by Hayward Gallery Publishing,
London SE1 8XX
© The South Bank Centre 1998
Essay © Nick Groom 1998

ISBN 1 85332 187 7

National Touring Exhibitions, Hayward Gallery and Arts Council Collection publications are distributed by Cornerhouse Publications, 70 Oxford Street, Manchester M1 5NH (tel. 0161 200 1503; fax. 0161 237 1504).

# Preface

Exhibitions curated by artists are an important element of our National Touring Exhibitions programme and have produced some of the most stimulating projects of recent years. The artist's enquiring spirit and eye can unlock habitual assumptions about the presentation of works of art and the conventions of exhibitions. Artists as curators invariably interpret the task of making an exhibition as an extension of their own practice, and for this reason the results are doubly interesting: both in themselves and for the light they shed on the artist's work.

Richard Wentworth's art is informed by an acute awareness of the peculiarities and potency of everyday objects, and the resonances between things of different categories and media. *Thinking Aloud* brings together an extraordinary range of objects from many spheres. We are immensely grateful to Richard Wentworth for the imagination, wit and energy that he has brought to the project, as well as for his dedication and enthusiasm.

It is appropriate that *Thinking Aloud* opens at Kettle's Yard, whose Director Michael Harrison has been in dialogue with the artist for many years. We appreciate the commitment that he and our colleagues, Paul Bailey at Cornerhouse and Jenni Lomax at Camden Arts Centre, have made to it from its beginnings. The exhibition is intended to grow from showing to showing, with new works and different formations. Because of its evolving and unpredictable nature, it is impossible to represent it fully in this book, which has been conceived as a parallel undertaking with its own rationale. We thank Nick Groom for his inspired essay and Herman Lelie for a design that matches so well the artist's wishes. Lucy Head contributed essential research. I remain grateful too to Roger Malbert, the Hayward's NTE Senior Curator, for his creative engagement with the project.

We thank the artists and lenders for their generosity, and the following for their help and advice: Hugh Aldersey-Williams, Hugh Allan, Leo Bessant, Glyn Biesty, Dr Tim Bliss, Ron Brooker, Gordon Burn, Magda Carneci, Robin Cooper, Paul Cornish, Lisa Corrin, Sinzina Dragos, Caroline Dale Kobayashi, Stephen Dalken, Joanna Drew, Brian Durrans, James Dyson, Gordon Edington, Tom Emerson, Robin Fletcher, Peter de Francia, Teresa Gleadowe, Ralph Goodwin, Kit Grover, Michael Harrison, Suzie Joel, Penny Johnson, Linda Karshan, Derek Kinsella, Maite Lorés, Jenni Lomax, Sheila Mackie, Michael Moody, Gregor Muir, Herbie Müller, Hoda el Naggar, Charles Newton, Jo O'Driscoll, Sue Osborne, Raj Pal, Mike Parsons, Sara Pimpaneau, Emma and Sarah Posey, Jurrie Poot, James Putnam, Jonathan Riddell, Julian Rothenstein, Janet Skidmore, Sally Tallant, Peter Thomas, Cathy du Toit, Roger Tolson, Jude Tyrrell, Marina Warner, Jack Wendler, Angela Weight, Jane, Joe and Felix Wentworth, Sarah Wilson and John Wyver.

**Susan Ferleger Brades**
Director, Hayward Gallery

# Introduction

## Roger Malbert

The title *Thinking Aloud* suggests spontaneity and perhaps a certain level of freedom
or irresponsibility. The surrealists argued for thought that was 'made in the mouth'
and Erasmus, in *Praise of Folly*, attaches similar value to saying 'what first comes to
mind'. The spark of inspiration is an old idea, and while the surrealist faith in
the unconscious as a source of revelation may be outmoded today, it is not difficult
to appreciate the special energy of first thoughts, scribbled in haste on the back of
an envelope*, or swiftly sketched or modelled by hand out of primitive materials. Such
moments provide the starting point for *Thinking Aloud*; but they are not its only
subject. To think aloud is either to muse in solitude or confide in one's (presumably
sympathetic) listener. It is a provisional mode of discourse, in which ideas can be tested,
contradicted or rearranged. The act of thinking aloud is a metaphor here for the
process of composing an exhibition and among its various themes is the nature of
the exhibition itself, as a medium of communication and artistic practice.

It could be argued that the art of exhibition-making is still in its infancy. Exhibitions
are ephemeral and their history – in the manner of oral histories – is elusive and
subject to the vagaries of memory. Documentation rarely amounts to more than a few
photographs which, however evocative, convey only a partial impression of the event
as it would have been experienced in time and space. Catalogues, even when they
include actual installation shots, provide an equally imperfect record. The most
influential models of exhibition therefore tend to be the least adventurous and risk-
taking: the permanent – or semi-permanent – displays in museums. This may be why
contemporary curatorial practice – increasingly professionalised and self-consciously
'critical' – remains steeped in convention; the museum posits standards, not simply
those determined by a necessary concern for the safety of the exhibits but also less
explicit values of historical judgement and aesthetic decorum.

By contrast with such claims to professional authority, the artist-curated exhibition
is likely to be declaredly subjective, resisting historical orthodoxies and academic
specialisms. For Richard Wentworth, those curatorial certainties would be of doubtful
value, just as a narrow, unambiguous fixity of purpose would be inappropriate for

the creation of art. Like a work of art, an exhibition can be complex, ironic and contradictory. It can be provisional, acknowledging freely in its informal arrangement of things that it could be otherwise. It may also disrupt that 'tidy-mindedness' that would declare a *cordon sanitaire* around the domain of art, and exclude from it all other categories of object.

A certain cautious informality is in fact a hidden feature of most exhibitions of art, other than those prescribed by chronology or other logical considerations. The 'hang', the installation, is a moment of necessary spontaneity, where unforeseen effects are produced as soon as objects are positioned in space. It is a version of the creative process, speculative and personal. Then, when the arrangement is settled and declared to be definitive (it cannot be bettered), art becomes public, like thoughts committed to paper – and is exposed to the critical gaze.

* Charles Newton's exhibition at the Victorian & Albert Museum, *The Back of the Envelope: First Thoughts in Design*, 1996, explored this territory and was a point of departure for *Thinking Aloud*.

# Thoughts on Paper

**Richard Wentworth, prompted and transcribed by Roger Malbert**

**Malbert** This could be seen as an argumentative exhibition, with its eclectic choices and provocative juxtapositions of disparate items, yet there is obviously not just one point that is being made. Could you say something about the complexity of the show you have assembled. What was your approach in forming it?

**Wentworth** In thinking about arrangements of things, I would want to make a distinction between display and exhibition. Display is an essential aspect of urban life. We are surrounded by display, every shop window is a theatrical space, with things arranged in it for effect. Parked cars are display. In the over-developed landscape that we all inhabit it's hard not to attribute some intention to everything that we survey.

An art exhibition is a genre of a related activity. It's a particularly refined effort, set apart in its own exclusion zone, as it usually is. The gallery is an ambiguous place in our culture. There's a code for entering it; it's a space somewhere between a library and a shop. Things are laid out for you as they are in a shop, but there's the possibility of research, of each person exploring it in their own way. But there's a threshold to overcome. You don't wander into a gallery by accident. It's like certain kinds of shops that one would never go into, because they're too specialist or exclusive.

**M** So once you've overcome those obstacles and entered the gallery, would you say that there is a certain predictability in the way that art is presented?

**W** One of the pleasures of entering an exhibition space is the way it changes our mind-set, something we anticipate when we set out but that only happens when the world drops away at the door. The entrance, though, is permeable. We have all had the experience of being in galleries with windows which offer us views back into the world. That, or the mere presence of other visitors in the gallery of different types and ages is enough of a reminder of the diverse points of view that exhibitions generate.

**M** How do you reconcile that delicate experience of looking at art in a gallery with the world outside?

**W** In the street we are used to a confusion of images, messages and signs, and we're able to deal with this extraordinary variety of levels of expression of power and value.

We're mostly able to navigate, making decisions, avoiding getting run over, noticing and making sense of things, editing them in our own way. What I like about the city is this – that what is threatening to one person is wallpaper to the next. So why shouldn't we be able to accept a similar variety of contradictions in an exhibition, to manage the diversity and enjoy the fact that our experience is not the same as the next person's?

**M** What principles, aesthetic or otherwise, have governed your choice of things and your decisions about their arrangement?

**W** Various threads run through the exhibition, questions of size and scale, of how we give meaning to things, how we share value, how thoughts become ideas become realities. Some canons we are happy enough to agree upon, others we prefer to debate – perhaps endlessly.

Lurking amongst all the material is the imponderable notion of 'resonance', the way certain things seem to chime. Resonance and association are among the least explicable aspects of our lives, but we'd never make a move without them. There are some mythic stories in the history of science, celebrating such moments of recognition: Harry Kroto's understanding of Carbon 60 for example, was accelerated by his fond memories of Buckminster Fuller's dome structures, which he'd first seen as a young man.

**M** That kind of fortuitous or unconscious association is not necessarily apparent in the finished work, without background knowledge. In *Thinking Aloud* you have included a number of finished pieces by contemporary artists. Do these have a different status because of the artist's intention? What is their relation to the sketches and maquettes, which are full of potential and incomplete, or to the other things, manufactured and found objects?

**W** After a century of mass overproduction, terms like 'found object', or the exquisitely dignified *objet trouvé*, are obsolete. Whoever first said 'readymade' was very clever, but it's a long time since people discovered that you could dig with an antler – something serviceable, heraldic and mythic all rolled into one. Humans don't change that much.

Léger has that great story of going with Brancusi and Duchamp to the Salon d'Aviation in 1913. Duchamp is eyeing a propellor and turns to Brancusi and says, 'Painting is finished'. Actually art has always been *in the world* and is perfectly able to look after itself. We like to discriminate, but if you can't relax your discrimination there's no room to move. A convenient popular falsehood has art existing in hermetic groupings – grouped by age, gender, nationality, materials. Fortunately culture is much stranger than that and if art is any good it eludes type-casting. The artworks in *Thinking Aloud* were made at different times in the twentieth century with quite different motives.

I'd like to think of the exhibition in conversational terms, appealing to the viewer's curiosity, drawing on the fact that we are all inquisitive. In conversation we are quickly aware of someone's tastes and appetites; we give something back, and in this exchange a threshold is crossed. I am not interested in being illustrative or didactic. Part of the predicament in presenting a show is to keep this fluidity and open-endedness, where meanings are fugitive and things can coalesce in different ways. I think there is often a spurious authority at work in exhibitions, where the label dictates to the viewer and narrows the margins for an individual response. This is not about claiming territory or owning ideas.

*Thinking Aloud* is an opportunity to see what happens if you fray the edges and actually provoke more open-ended ways of looking: something that cannot be tested on paper or CAD mock-up, but can only be given form and experienced in the space itself. Like art it doesn't exist until it has an audience, until it's populated, tried and tested.

**M** Perhaps it would be helpful to talk about some examples from your selection. The project began with your enquiry into 'first thoughts', sketches and models?

**W** When I saw Frank Gehry's 1995 show in Venice of his models and drawings for the Bilbao Guggenheim, what I found thrilling was that there seemed to be a very stark gap between the rough sketches and process models, with their energy and sense of the pleasure of messing about with form and devising ways in which that form could be articulated and changed and made habitable, and the finished computerised models. When you see the two side by side you appreciate that imaginative trajectory, from the mundane activity of making something with your hands, in the same way that children do, out of a Corn Flakes packet – and believing it – to the presentation model or drawing. These initial workings out of ideas can be ugly or crude, you don't criticise them for that, because their first aim is not to please but to find something out.

Paxton's Crystal Palace drawing, which is so spectacularly immediate, is an earlier example. It's impossible for us to imagine the confidence of that entrepeneurial moment of the 1840s – when you look at that drawing, which is clearly someone speaking to himself, you can't imagine that he was anticipating that it would actually be built. You invest the drawing retrospectively with huge import, because it actually is the first conceptualisation of the 1851 Great Exhibition.

**M** At the other extreme from that optimistic moment is the Great Depression of the 1930s, recorded by Walker Evans in his photographs for the Farm Security Administration. These clearly have a particular significance for you.

**W** Well, in thinking about the American influence on British culture, it seems to me that we are caught between all those European languages that most of us don't speak and America, to which through the accident of a shared language, we have a false sense of access. For people of my generation, who have felt the blur of that influence especially strongly, our reach on the history of this century extends back perhaps as far as the Depression. That's just about obtainable, as opposed to World War One which seems very far away. Walker Evans' famous pictures of cotton share croppers and small town life and soil erosion on Mississippi farmland during that time are really photos of failure, of that hugely powerful and beautiful country in hopeless despair. In these pictures what is instantly legible is the architectonic underpinning – the rows and grids, which give an incredibly powerful feeling of the regulation of space in America. They really are sculptural photographs, they convey how the world is ordered, physically; how America got started, with this mapping out of the land both for farms and for cities. The geometry of North America is pretty bizarre. Apparently, it was Jefferson in 1785 who put the straight lines in America – essentially a device for surveying and selling land, a European-inspired template dropped onto a 'blank' continent.

**M** Maps, relief models and plans are other ways of representing the land, and.you have included a great variety of these, from a war-time briefing model to ironic variations on these themes by contemporary artists.

**W** A map is, along with writing, one of our earliest ways of finding our way around in the world. The level of performance in maps varies enormously, depending on the information they're supposed to provide. From the simple sketch showing you how to get to the post office around the corner, it's a huge leap to the map showing where Vladivostock is in relation to Istanbul. There's also an intermediate space where the map can be decorative, and we use old maps in this way: when the demarcations of areas they show become outmoded, they become pictures to hang on the wall. Mariele Neudecker plays with this discrepancy between the objective certitude of official maps and people's private, idiosyncratic conceptions of how the world is.

The twentieth century will probably be remembered for its flatness, its obsession with the smooth, with surface, with shine. The perfecting of the map, the survey, as forms of idealisation, is obviously implicated in this. All these qualities are found in airfields: flatness and straightness erasing the landscape. Ariel photographs taken from a perfect point of view directly above Heathrow show it as a diagram of itself. It could be taken for a military site, which is exactly what it was previously. Frankfurt airport is famous for being both simultaneously civil and military.

**M** You love foraging and this exhibition has given you an excuse to investigate some collections, most notably the Imperial War Museum's. Military imagery occurs in *Thinking Aloud* in various forms, and I suspect that there might have been more, as you began to sift through the Museum's extraordinary photographic archives.

**W** In looking at reportage and documentary photography I recognise a process in myself; I wander, picking up incidentals of texture, perfectly mindful of how photographs are inseparable from their points of view, not thinking of them as reality but nonetheless travelling through an approximation of their historical and geographical moment. I was born half-way through a century that has devoted enormous energy to this way of seeing things, so it must have affected me greatly. All this visibility, though, is not transparency. All the really big agencies in our lives are shrouded in secrecy: politics and government, the judiciary etc.

There's a way in which I feel the military is central to all this, barely visible but infinitely affecting – the true complexity of the relationship between the military and industrial; America's roads are 'Defense Highways' (ours are 'Roman'). There's something about the enormous scale of it all, mostly invisible of course (codebreakers invent computers and it shouldn't surprise us that this is where the internet originated). What drives these things from notion to reality? The built-in obsolescence of the process, the principle that everything will always be superseded. There is nothing quite so pathetic as the discards of the military, of 'Government surplus'. You can stretch this further by visiting, say, the remains of an Iron Age hill fort, which is only a little more redundant than the American airbase at Greenham Common.

Contrast this with the political rage that was spontaneously articulated hundreds of times when Romanians tore out the emblem of the Socialist Republic from the centre of their flag – a completely new image was created, a heraldry of absence. This, for me, is a paramount example of a public sculpture which necessitated destroying a painting – in this case a flag. It's humbling to think of art in such company, but it's the kind of expression that artists recognise – one way among many that reminds them how demanding the project is.

**M** The Patent Office represents another system of social regulation of production. This like the IWM was a place you were clearly excited to visit.

**W** There's a strange parallel between the kinds of *absolute* which the military strives for – and fails to achieve – and the impulse to make art. In part, artists criticise their previous work by making more work. It's easy to understand the impetus for art but difficult to understand the procedure, the shift from private speculative activity to resolution under the public gaze. Once a great work of art or architecture exists it feels absolute, it has a sense of inevitability.

Patents are making a play for some sort of necessity. Like art they grow out of a speculative activity, a proposal of adventure or discovery. When you look at a lot of patents you think how amazing that there's this legal sieve through which they must all pass. A proposal enters the patent office and becomes definitive. You can imagine a patent office for art, where ideas are registered, experiences logged – but it wouldn't be art.

Perhaps also it's the implicit role of secrecy and subterfuge for the military which corresponds to the legal protection that a patent is supposed to grant. Art, which originates in extreme privacy travels by a very different route. Art is absorbent but it's also a leaky thing and if it's any good it seeps out into a wider consciousness where it gets measured. The simultaneous attraction and terror of seeing art tested out before a public is one of its most exhilarating moments. Exhibitions are sites of condensation, transitory opportunities to take a reading. I really dislike the way that people refer to 'the public' as if it were a single unified entity. There are many different publics, variously motivated, who might desire something from this kind of exchange. Some have very clear rules of engagement, others are up for a much more speculative game, and art is simultaneously moulded and deformed under their gazes.

There's a gap between what we recognise as intended and what we dismiss as accidental. It's an ambiguity I'm particularly drawn to. There is an obvious foil to it – all of those things that have been made in the name of 'servicibility' which ricochet and make images – methods of tilling which come to define landscapes and characterise property rights, etc, or Crusoe stumbling on plant propagation by the accident of his fortification method: his stakes took root and sprang to life.

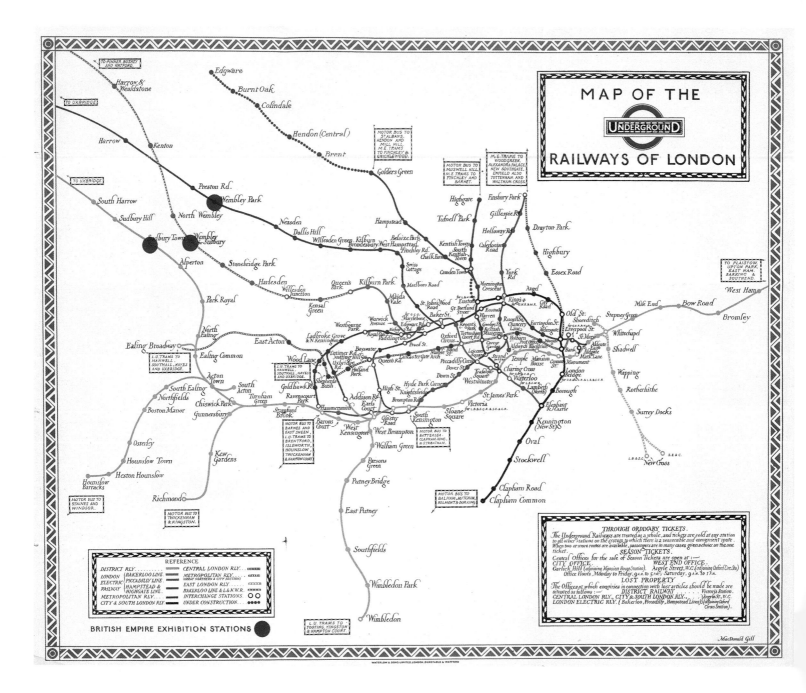

## MAP OF THE UNDERGROUND RAILWAYS OF LONDON

MacDonald Gill

**BRITISH EMPIRE EXHIBITION STATIONS** ●

### REFERENCE

| | |
|---|---|
| DISTRICT RLY. | CENTRAL LONDON RLY. |
| LONDON { BAKERLOO LINE | METROPOLITAN RLY. (GREAT NORTHERN & CITY SECTION) |
| ELECTRIC { PICCADILLY LINE | EAST LONDON RLY. |
| RAILWAY { HAMPSTEAD & HIGHGATE LINE | BAKERLOO LINE & L.&N.W.R. |
| METROPOLITAN RLY. | INTERCHANGE STATIONS ○○ |
| CITY & SOUTH LONDON RLY. | UNDER CONSTRUCTION |

### THROUGH ORDINARY TICKETS.
The Underground Railways are treated as a whole, and tickets are sold at any station to all other Stations on the system, to which there is a reasonable and convenient route. When two or more routes are available, passengers are in many cases given a choice on the one ticket.

### SEASON TICKETS.
Central Offices for the sale of Season Tickets are open at:—
CITY OFFICE, WEST END OFFICE.
Garlick Hill (adjoining Mansion House Station). Argyle Street, W.C. (adjoining Oxford Circ. Sta.)
Office Hours: Monday to Friday, 9 A.M. to 5 P.M.; Saturday, 9 A.M. to 1 P.M.

### LOST PROPERTY
The Offices at which enquiries in connection with lost articles should be made are situated as follows:—
DISTRICT RAILWAY .. Victoria Station.
CENTRAL LONDON RLY., CITY & SOUTH LONDON RLY. .. Argyle St., W.C.
LONDON ELECTRIC RLY. (Bakerloo, Piccadilly, Hampstead Lines) (adjoining Oxford Circus Station).

WATERLOW & SONS LIMITED, LONDON, DUNSTABLE & WATFORD

**2**

case '97 – okt.

3

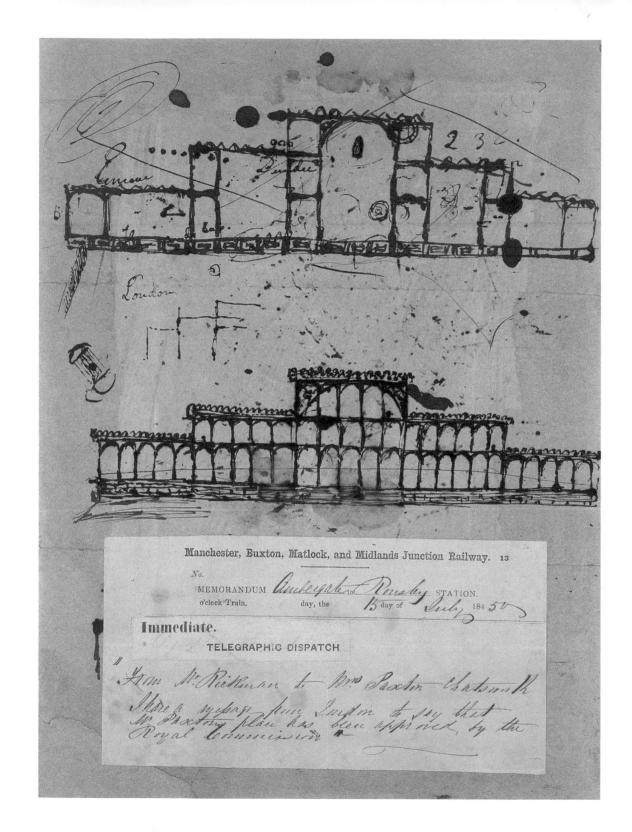

Manchester, Buxton, Matlock, and Midlands Junction Railway. 13

No.

MEMORANDUM *Ambergate* to *Rowsley* STATION.

o'clock Train,           day, the           15 day of *July* 184 5

**Immediate.**

TELEGRAPHIC DISPATCH

"From Mr Rickman to Mrs Paxton Chatsworth I have a message from London to say that Mr Paxton's plan has been approved by the Royal Commission"

8

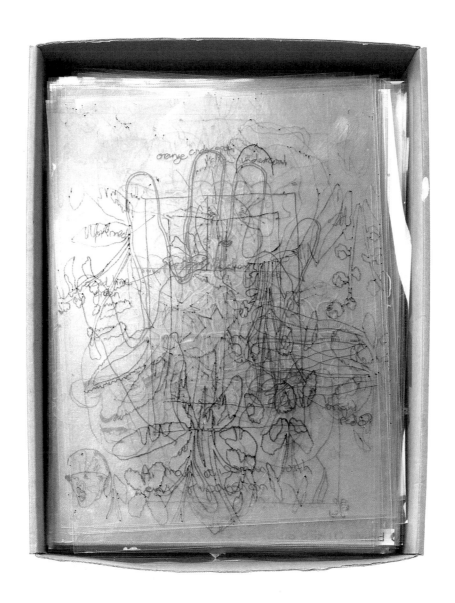

DIANA • THE PEOPLES PRINCESS • 1961-1997

10

# An Artist's Manual

**Nick Groom**

### What is this? Stuff?

Richard Wentworth's thinking aloud:

> *A sort of Thesaurus of objects has arisen… How do we find a pen which suits us? What is a favourite pair of shoes, and must they 'fit'?… How do artists find a way with things, reject, choose, feel 'right' about something, how do they criticise their choice… And have you ever looked up 'thesaurus' in the Thesaurus…?*

This essay traces the hand and the eye of Richard Wentworth in *Thinking Aloud*, and offers some thoughts on how his questions might be answered. It is a collaborative effort – the artist's words and phrases and examples resonate through the following pages, sometimes italicised to emphasise the conversational and co-operative nature of the enterprise, but more often silent, secret, covert – because while I agree that *Thinking Aloud* is Wentworth's *fault*, it is not necessarily his *responsibility…*[1] Neither is this an existential, or a semiological, or a materialist analysis of the life of objects, for I have tried to avoid derelict systems of thought. Rather, the objects gathered here constitute a freewheeling argument, an animated conversation, and show that building an exhibition is, in the context of Richard Wentworth's activity, an artistic practice.

Richard Wentworth does not approach objects straightforwardly; he unlocks the relationship of body and material, *unpacks* physical metaphors with oblique strategies. He collects shopping lists – but only when he finds them, through *hasard objectif*, discarded in the gutter, *'as part of the moment'*. *Thinking Aloud* takes its inspiration from such debris: lists culled and salvaged and made into other lists, maps and measurements for navigating the topographies of our ground. The ground we inhabit today is that of the urban, but it is composed from the throwaways of the past: we dwell on what archaeologists call *made ground*.

> *We are all accumulation.*

20 mm

13

## Here & There

A book, found in a junk shop, produced 'in complete conformity' with the War Economy Standard, compressed by a third: 'in order to save paper… margins have been reduced and no space has been wasted between chapters'. The words, like fingers in a glove, fit the page snugly. The book has a manual quality, an economy, a management, a tight grip of meaning on the page, a narrative utility. It is a functional book; occasional dog-ears show the flight and rest of previous readers, and as a story it works. And yet, it was plucked, by hand, from a bale of dying books that tomorrow – the day after – would have been spirited away by dustmen. These works are evanescent, they are melting away; they are crossing the narrowed margin of materiality into nothingness. The reader of such books gathers rather than hunts, finds rather than seeks. And reads in any order.

## Drift

Objects drift, and leave tracks and traces of history and character; sometimes they drift together and chime and seem to conduct secrets. Sometimes these properties lie in the future, as studies or plans, maquettes or prototypes:

> a Frank Gehry design process model, Paxton's preliminary sketch for the Great Exhibition building, a Hoover cannibalised by James Dyson for his own vacuum cleaner design, Lutyens's initial sketches for the Cenotaph or Lloyd George's fugue-like doodle on his blotting paper at the signing of the Armistice;

or these properties lie in blueprints, patents (the flip-top cigarette packet), templates, or moulds. Or perhaps properties inhabit the parallel perspective of the photograph: the surveyed landscapes of Walker Evans, the Bechers' inventories of industrial architecture, or Andreas Gursky's endless uniform lattices of cellular living. Or again, properties are embodied in definitive weights and measures, masters, jigs, and tools, in moulds for rubbers and gold (tyres and condoms and ingots), in maps and charts or a briefing model for the D-Day landings, in memorials of the white cliffs of Dover, memory maps of the world, and sometimes mapping the intimacies of the body in prosthetic limbs or body bags. Or properties dwell in silence: a packing case tailored for a sculpture, a Julian Opie vacant landscape, a Romanian flag with the centre cut out (from the 1989 revolution), a painting of a drifting mine, a toy model of an explosion…

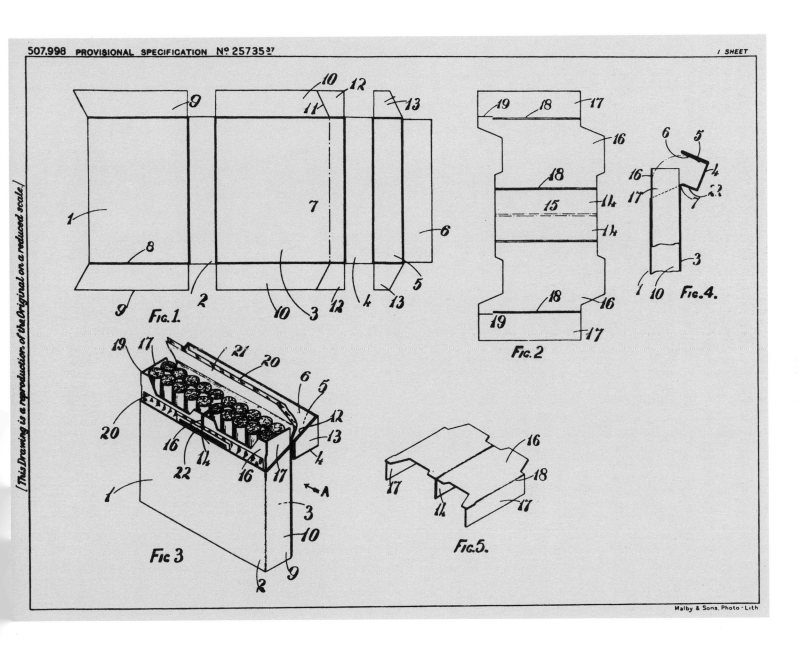

Fig.1.

Fig.2

Fig.4.

Fig 3

Fig.5.

15

## Tread

Traces remain, however, of certain invisible yet complicit routes around these objects. From airport departure lounges to motorway service stations, there are holes in carpets, holes where travellers stand to gaze out of windows at the slick surfaces of tarmac or sky, holes where itchy feet have pawed the pile, holes that map anticipation and expectation, holes where meaning seeps in. These sidelong trips from coffee-machine to window to reverie are like any interactive movement through any room, any city, any art gallery, any collection. They shape the space and leave marks, like flags, or clues.

> *I think there's a particular dynamism in a show when you see something over there that then makes you cross the space in some specific way.*

So *Thinking Aloud* is not a collection or an archive; it offers no totalising classification, but a series of trajectories that lace across each other. The reader too takes lines of flight. There are no neat fits here – but everything might fit, from *that* perspective. The mysterious properties of objects are deliberately exaggerated by presenting 'first thoughts', blueprints, models, and maps. Indeed as in a railway system, objects only exist in circulation and connection, and, as in *The Great Bear*, lines *'really sing where they cross'*. Our journey is not arborescent; we can pursue any number of routes in a tangled skein. Knowledge does not grow on trees here – and neither does it grow *like* trees. It seeps and spreads, in drifts and *derives*, pulled by radar and magnets.

## Trail

Maps, meanwhile, colonise and explicate, they make the world legible in the most unrolled, explicit terms, to replace the real with signs and make themselves the territory. They impose upon the fractal coastline and justify the margin. They paint a picture that has pretensions to be a template. Cartography is the most hegemonic of the arts, and its rhetoric of co-ordinates and grids and routes and contours is a device for locking land in place, for overcoming land.

> ... In that Empire, the Art of Cartography reached such Perfection that the map of one Province alone took up the whole of a City, and the map of the empire, the whole of a Province. In time, those Unconscionable Maps did not satisfy and the Colleges of Cartographers set up a Map of the Empire which had the size of the Empire itself and coincided with it point by point...

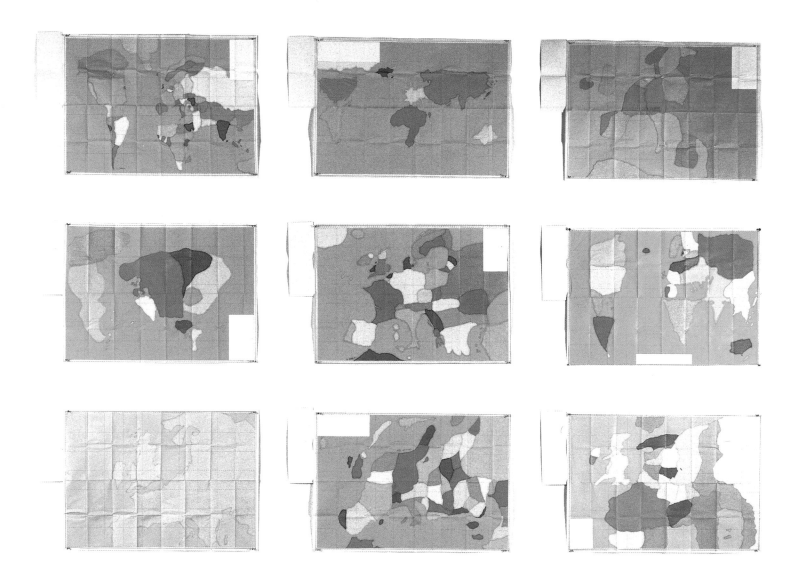

17

Megemlékezésül
Esztergom, szabad királyi
városból, a trianoni
határon fekvő ma-
gyar Róma, a régi
királyi szék helyről.
1937 évi szeptember 29.

városi tanácsnok

Igazolom, hogy a Magyar Diáljáloи se a
mai napon Budapest székesfőváros polgár-
hivatalából jelentkezett
Budapest 1937 okt. 1.
a polgármester rendeletéből.
fővárosi

Succeeding generations, however, abandon this 'Widespread Map':

> In the deserts of the West some mangled Ruins of the Map lasted on, inhabited
> by Animals and Beggars; in the whole Country there are no other relics of the
> Disciplines of Geography.[2]

## Index

Unpick a map and you are left with a list – alphabeticised street names, road numbers,
trig points. List-making is constitutive of order, a freezing point that solidifies
the world and makes it stable: placing objects in a list transforms them into orderly
little graphemes arranged in a linear procession, stamps in an album, works of art
in a gallery. And yet lists are leaky, and things in lists are promiscuous – risking hybrid
relationships with their neighbours (the librarian finds John Bunyan nestling up against
Angela Carter; the art historian finds Dada before Dadd; in a dictionary 'exhibit'
is succeeded by 'exhilarate'). So, despite being an extreme model of order, lists may
yet threaten to evacuate meaning altogether, like a siren of nonsense. Even short lists
like 'from A to B' or 'hocus-pocus' have this meaningless charm, this chime, this
jingle-jangle. List-making becomes an enchantment – and an illusion. The enumeration
of Eusthenes, who spelled out his satisfaction, is entrancing:

> I am no longer hungry. Until the morrow, safe from my saliva all the following shall be:
> Aspics, Acalephs, Acanthocephalates, Amoebocytes, Ammonites, Axolotls, Amblystomas,
> Aphisilions, Anacondas, Ascarids, Amphisbaenas, Angleworms, Amphipods, Anaerobes,
> Annelids, Anthozoans...[3]

This list is additive and addictive. We could add, add, add forever – and should at least
add the Adder. When are there words enough? When is the lexicon full, and how do we
then choose?

## Waves

List-making has co-ordination too. We can rethread lists as maps, as a form of seeing
or image-making. '*I am nearly incapable of not seeing*', says Richard Wentworth,
discussing his photographic archive 'Making Do and Getting By':

> *I record things as if I were trying to fix the visual weather. I don't file these pictures
> or order them, I don't look at them for pleasure or analysis; so they are almost like biologist's
> slides – slides of thoughts visible only when illuminated...*

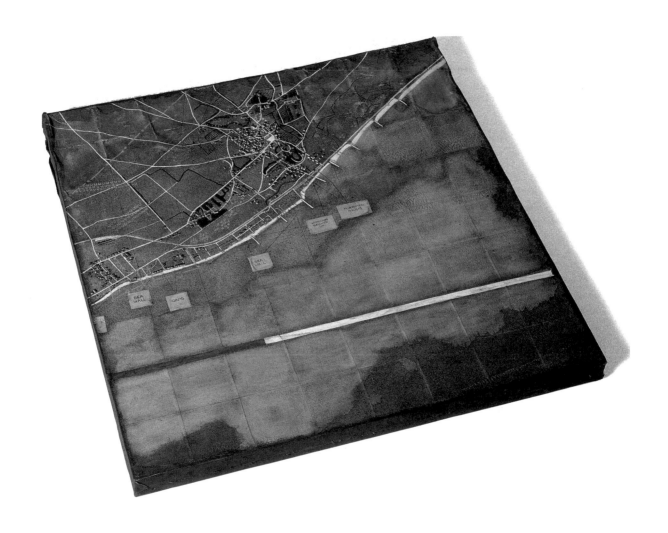

20

# Thinking Aloud

Vladimir Archipov
Questionnaire, 1998
Courtesy Teresa Gleadowe

Assorted patents
specifications and illustrations
The Patent Office, London

2 bales of scrap metal
Aluminium 1.82 kg
Steel 3.18 kg
Richard Freeth Recycling

Margaret Barron
Finchley Road, 1999
oil paint on adhesive tape
Courtesy of the artist

Basil Beattie
This and That, 1991-1997
71 individual drawings, chinese ink on paper
Courtesy of the artist

'The Blue Book'
The Blue Book lists all 400 routes which a London
cab driver must learn while 'doing the knowledge'
Courtesy the Public Carriage Office

Mel Bochner
Estimating an 8" x 8" Square, 1972
pencil/coloured pencil on paper
Private collection, London

Mel Bochner
Estimating an 8" x 8" Square, 1972
pencil/coloured pencil on paper
Private collection, London

'Carnes' prosthetic hand, c.1914-17
metal
Courtesy Robin Cooper, Steeper Ltd

'Celebrate the Century'
sheet of stamps with verso bearing explanatory
texts, 1999
Courtesy of Lucy Sisman

Collapsible ladder
contemporary French

Colour Atlas (x 2)
Broken Books – George Hardie 1997
edition of 50

Conversational sketch to illustrate the footprint
of a new art gallery, November 1998
photocopy (Milton Keynes Gallery Director's
left palm)
Stephen Snoddy

Keith Coventry
Untitled (Kebab Sculpture No. 1), 1998
bronze with electric motor on plinth
The artist, courtesy Richard Salmon Gallery

Keith Coventry
(White Abstract) Winston Churchill,
after Graham Sutherland, 1995
oil on canvas
Courtesy Christie's Corporate Art Collection

Double Canted Brick Die
cast iron
Baggeridge Brick plc

Marcel Duchamp
'Don't Forget'
specimen signature supplied to Richard Hamilton
Collection Richard Hamilton

Dummy rifle
Training aid, Eton College, early 20th century
softwood

Peter Fischli / David Weiss
Der Lauf der Dinge, 1987/88
video: running time: 30 minutes
Courtesy Mick Kerr

Flag on moon simulating wind
'Life' Magazine
8 September 1969

Dan Flavin
Ceiling/Wall/Floor, 1970
ballpoint pen on paper
Private collection, London

Anya Gallaccio
Remains from 'Broken English' project, 1991/97
photo booth photographs
Courtesy of the artist

Kit Grover
'Mushroom Cloud', 1998
childhood recollection – letter to RW
Courtesy of the artist

Philip Guston
Alcove, 1969
oil on board
Private collection

Philip Guston
August Form, 1964
oil on paper
Private collection, London

Hazard warning signs
1 German, 2 British, 1 Spanish, 1 Belgian, 2 French

Heathrow, aerial photographs, 1949, 1959, 1988,
1996
Courtesy British Airport Authority

Hooded cape in waterproof camouflage material,
1992
Swiss military

Hunter's gloves
'Superflauge', contemporary American

Hunter's veil
'Superflauge', contemporary American

36" Imperial measure
carpenter's folding rule with Braille numerals

Kendal and Dent's Time Chart of the World
Courtesy John Carpenter

Peter Kennard
All Clear: Greater London Council poster, 1970s
photolithograph on paper
Imperial War Museum, London

Bob Law
Looking to Calais from Abbots Cliff, 1992
pencil on paper
The artist, courtesy Marlene Eleini

Bob Law
Looking to France from Sandgate Esplanade,
September 1992
pencil on paper
The artist, courtesy Marlene Eleini

Bob Law
Untitled, 22 January 1963
pencil on paper
The artist, courtesy Marlene Eleini

Brighid Lowe
Truth-Hallucinations (no. 1), 1996-97
c-type
University of Southampton, John Hansard Gallery

Brighid Lowe
Truth-Hallucinations (no. 2), 1996-97
c-type
University of Southampton, John Hansard Gallery

Bigas Luna
Franco, 1975
photograph taken from British television shortly
before Franco's death
Private collection

Mackay split hook (prosthetic hand), c.1920s
steel
Courtesy Robin Cooper, Steeper Ltd

Make-believe small bore shot gun
early 1980s

Map showing all 400 routes and prominent
buildings which must be learned by licensed
London cab drivers
Courtesy Mr Howell, the Public Carriage Office

Charles Mason
Sleeve, 1999
wood and rubber
Courtesy of the artist

Meccano Submarine
origin unknown
Private collection

'Mobile Phone calls prohibited'
Canadian sign

Pieter Laurens Mol
Oval Composition – According to the Laws of Chance
paper, glass/ black & white photograph, pencil
Stedelijk Museum, Amsterdam

Bruce Nauman
Modern (production) slant stool, 1966
'Small editions – cast in fibreglass'
pencil on paper
Private collection, London

Obsolete British bank notes in pelletised form
Courtesy Takako Hasegawa

Matt O'dell
"The Alfred P. Murrah Federal building in downtown Oklahoma City, site of Wednesday's car bombing that left at least 78 people dead and hundreds injured or missing", 1998
card and glue
Courtesy of the artist

Claes Oldenburg
proposed Monument for the Intersection of Canal Street and Broadway, New York: Block of Concrete Inscribed with the Names of War Heroes, 1965
Photocopy of page 266 of Hayward Gallery catalogue, 'Claes Oldenburg: An Anthology', 1995

Charles Pears
'Dazzled', A Camouflaged Battleship: HMS Ramillies in a gale of wind, 1918
oil on canvas
Imperial War Museum, London

Georges Perec 1936-1982
'La Vie-Mode d'Emploi'
pub. Hachette 1978, 700 pp
165 mm x 110 mm, 308 grams
'Life – A User's Manual'
pub. Collins Harvill 1987, 588 pp
translated David Bellos
215mm x 135 mm, 656 grams
Courtesy Tom Emerson

'Photography' magazine, October 1969
'The most photographed 30 seconds in History'
(Estimated nearly 50,000 exposures a second)

Sigmar Polke
Untitled, 1973
spray paint, glitter, wood on canvas
Private collection, London

Power figure (nkisi), 19th century
wood, nails
Kongo people, Central Africa
Horniman Museum and Public Gardens Trust

Kathy Prendergast
Ten City Drawings, 1994-98
Helsinki, Finland; Paris, France; Rome, Italy; Vilnius, Lithuania; Male, Maldives; Niamey, Niger; Castries, St Lucia; Kingstown, St Vincent; Bern, Switzerland; Washington, U.S.A
From the series '183 City Drawings'
pencil on paper
collection Irish Museum of Modern Art, Dublin

Proposal for re-arranging the map of London, using dummy lighting, 1918
Camouflage School, Kensington
Imperial War Museum, London

The Prosthesia hand
metal
Courtesy Robin Cooper, Hugh Steeper Ltd

Reconstructed head of King Midas of Phrygia, 1988
bronzed resin
The Manchester Museum, University of Manchester

Red Carpet
The choice of colour dates from the time of Imperial Rome, when it denoted dignity, power and strength. A red carpet is traditionally put out on special occasions to welcome important guests, royalty in particular, and acts as a form of low plinth.

Tom Sachs
12-Guage Shotgun, 1999
steel, painted softwood, etc
Courtesy of the artist

School Globe with elastic band and mapping pin as used by Francis Alÿs when proposing 'The Loop'
Collection Francis Alÿs

Helen Sharman
Transcript of Radio 4 Broadcast, 1996

Sheet of Princess Diana commemorative stamps printed 6th September 1997, face value £26, retail cost October 1998, £54

Roman Signer
Bett, 1996
ink-jet iris print
Private collection

Roman Signer
Preparatory drawings for projects, including: (bottom left) House with a flapping roof (Proposal for the 1999 Venice Biennale Swiss Pavilion Courtyard) and (centre left) A model helicopter approaching a pile of sand on a table – the sand is blown away revealing a lead ball which then rolls off the table.
Courtesy of the artist

William Smith (1769-1839)
Large-scale section of strata at Spofforth, ca. 1816
Oxford University Museum of Natural History, William Smith Archive

William Smith (1769-1839)
Section of strata … in the Fryerfold Vein … Old Gang Lead Mines, Swaledale, Yorks, 1819
Oxford University Museum of Natural History, William Smith Archive

William Smith (1769-1839)
Section of the veins of coal … in Lower and Upper Bilston Pits in the Forest of Dean, 1819
Oxford University Museum of Natural History, William Smith Archive

William Smith (1769-1839)
Westgarth Forster's section of the carboniferous and metalliferous strata, 1822
Oxford University Museum of Natural History, William Smith Archive

Standard Brick Die
cast iron
Baggeridge Brick plc

Simon Starling
Home-Made Eames, 1997
DKS chairs designed in 1955 by Charles Eames, Don Albinson and Dale Bauer and reproduced in two editions of six for B.C.C.
Block Collection

Simon Starling
Home-Made Eames (formas), 1997
DKS chairs designed in 1955 by Charles Eames, Don Albinson and Dale Bauer and reproduced in two editions of six for B.C.C.
Block Collection

The Steeper Scamp hand, 1995
Courtesy Robin Cooper, Steeper Ltd

Sun Study for Textured Gun Floors, 1918
Camouflage School, Kensington
Imperial War Museum, London

Tell-tale
installed 6 April 1999

Toy Mobile Phone with 6 functions

Toy tools, named and unnamed
injection-moulded plastic

Trenches in Kensington Gardens, north of the Serpentine, experimental site, WWI
2 balloon photographs
Camouflage School, Kensington
Imperial War Museum, London

'Vert Palombière'
1 litre pot of 'Hide Green' paint as used by French hunters

'The Wall That Heals'
– the travelling Vietnam Memorial
documentary photograph
Vietnam Veterans Memorial Fund
Photo by Holly Rotondi

Aby Warburg (d. 1929)
Mnemosyne Panels (Picture Atlas), late 1920s: one of the forty panels installed in Warburg's Rome apartment, and panel detail
Courtesy Warburg Institute

Keith Wilson
Football in Railings, 1998
iron railings, plastic football
Courtesy of the artist

*Performance:*

Pedro Moitinho
Nouns
performance installation – video monitors, desk, computer, fax machine, 30 metres of fax paper
8 – 11 April and 29 – 30 May 1999

Gary Stevens
Five-minute objects
Thursday 13 May 6.30-7.30

The metaphor of the weather is significant, replete with invisible forces (isobars and isotherms), and ubiquitous effects (wind and rain and sunshine). Meteorology struggles under continuous enumeration. The shipping forecast, like the index of an atlas (another place of disjuxtapositions), describes the point at which one form of representation ends and another begins:

> Dogger, Fisher, German Bight – mainly good; three to four rising. Biscay, South Finisterre, Shannon, Lundy, Fastnet, Irish Sea, Rockall, Malin, Hebrides – variable five, becoming cyclonic.

Word meets world, and, like two Johnsonian Englishmen, they converse about the weather. At the end of the world, at the edge of our imagination, are lists of clouds and inches of rain.

## List Awhile

Where might a list end? Variously constituted, it runs on madly, replotting itself like the notorious *Celestial Emporium of Benevolent Knowledge*, in which animals are divided into:

(a)   belonging to the Emperor,
(b)   embalmed,
(c)   tame,
(d)   sucking pigs,
(e)   sirens,
(f)   fabulous,
(g)   stray dogs,
(h)   included in the present classification,
(i)   frenzied,
(j)   innumerable,
(k)   drawn with a very fine camelhair brush,
(l)   *et cetera*,
(m)   having just broken the water pitcher,
(n)   that from a long way off look like flies…[4]

This list seems bent upon self-deconstruction, and also untwists the odder, more hectic order of the alphabet that meanders through this menagerie like stepping stones: a, b, c, d… The alphabet is made peculiar because it loses its integrity – but the alphabet is made in a peculiar fashion anyway: why does 'd' follow 'c' follow 'b' follow 'a'? This order of letters is the letter of the law, but it is a Keystone Cop version of the law, haring after runaway trains of letters and mischief-making words.

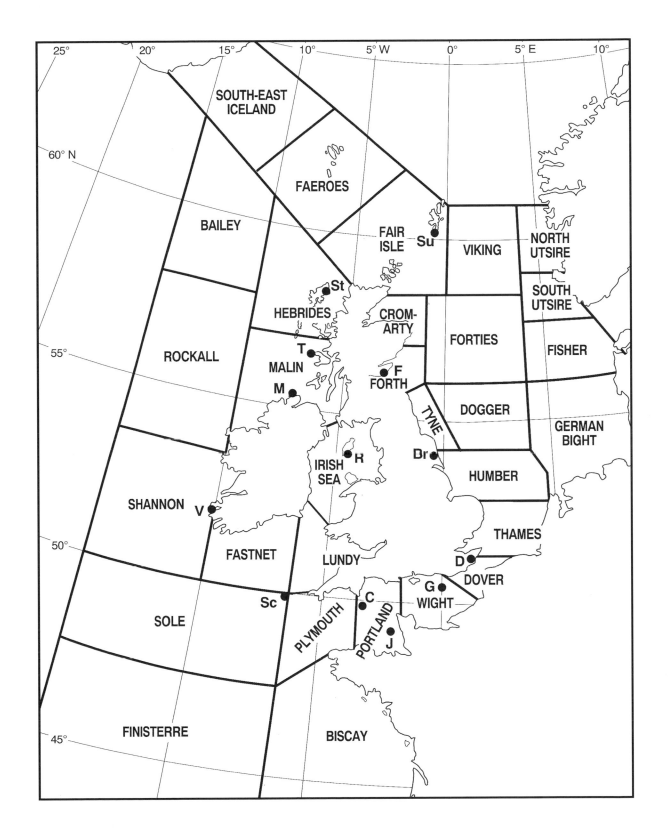

SOUTH-EAST ICELAND

FAEROES

BAILEY

FAIR ISLE   Su

VIKING

NORTH UTSIRE

SOUTH UTSIRE

St

HEBRIDES

CROM-ARTY

FORTIES

FISHER

ROCKALL

T

MALIN

M

F
FORTH

TYNE

DOGGER

GERMAN BIGHT

Dr

HUMBER

IRISH SEA

R

SHANNON   V

THAMES

D

FASTNET

LUNDY

DOVER

Sc

G

WIGHT

C

SOLE

PLYMOUTH

PORTLAND

J

FINISTERRE

BISCAY

25°
20°
15°
10°
5° W
0°
5° E
10°

60° N

55°

50°

45°

24

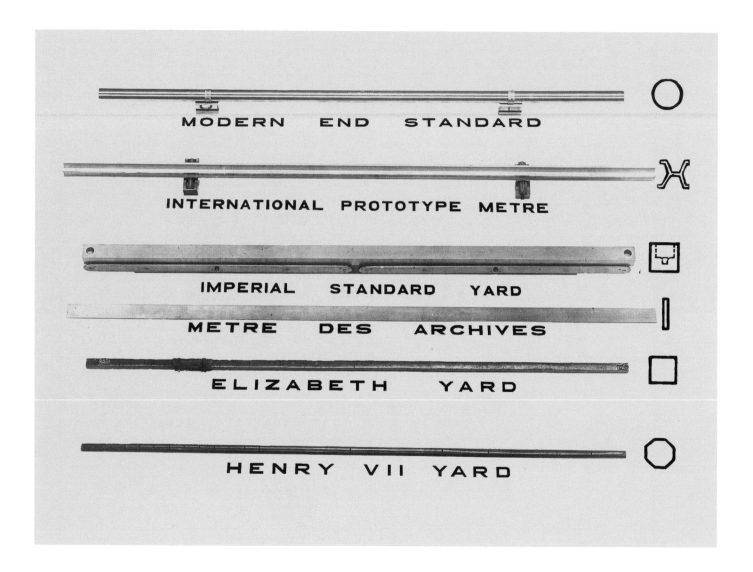

MODERN END STANDARD

INTERNATIONAL PROTOTYPE METRE

IMPERIAL STANDARD YARD

METRE DES ARCHIVES

ELIZABETH YARD

HENRY VII YARD

## Listless

Lists are made by arranging differences, and so formed in a sense by the signatures of objects. Each sign is discernible and each mark definable; there is no such thing as an unknown sign or a mute mark.[5] And so resemblances and differences become the units and limits of a list. Like letters in a word, they constitute a longer, meaningful signature; reflecting the acts of a body, *some*body. *Thinking Aloud* bears Richard Wentworth's signature, but illegibly. It is guided by his anatomies: the physical gesture, inflection, and sweep of the hand. It bears traces of work done and work still to be done. '*None of us leaves the world as we find it, but artists and criminals, perhaps, disturb it more wilfully.*' *Thinking Aloud* then is like a workshop or an inventory of tools and forms, or an artist's manual, in which Wentworth takes the role of a captivating surrealist patenter. Indeed, in the legal procedures of patenting, an idea is literally *reduced to art*, in the sense that 'reduction' means intensified or distilled, as a carcass is reduced to stock and stock is reduced to consommé. Thoughts, ideas, and schemes that are not *reduced to art* are consequently disadvantaged, as if they have not yet been properly shown. The precision tool is therefore *awaiting* its *reduction to art*, as if the patenter actually captures an intrinsic form. Conversely, these forms sometimes reach out to show themselves, some thoughts sit in similar fashions, sharing fabric and thread (even if the cut has altered), sometimes a rhyme sings out or a tone harmonises; and an eighteenth-century novel may chime with twentieth-century domestic surrealism.

## Sic

*Robinson Crusoe* is a thesaurus: book of lists, and a book about lists.[6] Once shipwrecked, Crusoe's list-making is epistemologically driven: to make sense of the island by naming each constituent part, and to eviscerate the remains of the ship in a long disentangling of itemised innards that provide for a new social order on the island. He starts emptying and dismantling the ship, retrieving a 'Carpenter's Cheft, two faws, an Axe, and a Hammer'. He is soon into the swing of *salvage*, a form of saving and salving, of material reaccumulation and reinvention. 'I believe verily, had the calm Weather held, I fhould have brought away the whole Ship Piece by Piece'.

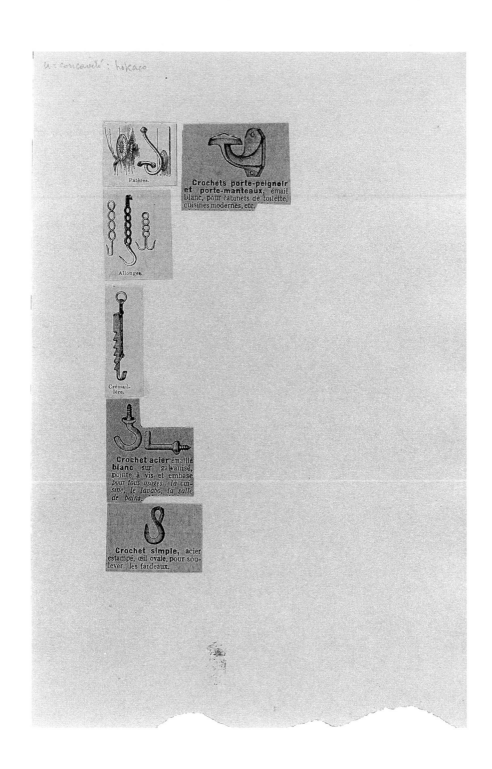

Patères.

Crochets porte-peignoir et porte-manteaux, émail blanc, pour cabinets de toilette, cuisines modernes, etc.

Allonges.

Crémaillère.

Crochet acier émaillé blanc sur galvanisé, pointe à vis et embase pour tous usages : la cuisine, le lavabo, la salle de bains.

Crochet simple, acier estampé, œil ovale, pour soulever les fardeaux.

## Item

Crusoe returns his deliberated flotsam and jetsam to compartments in his appropriately named 'Appartment' (he is apart…). Items are whisked out of drawers,

> two or three Razors, and one Pair of large Sizzers, with some ten or a Dozen of good Knives and Forks,

to disappear into chests and kegs, in his cave, within his walls. There's still more:

> Pens, Ink, Paper,… three or four Compaſſes, some Mathematical Inſtruments, Dials, Perſpectives, Charts, and Books of Navigation, all which I huddled together,… also I found three very good Bibles… a Dog and two Cats…

He returns to the wreck with an Iron Crow and 'got ſeveral Iron Bolts… I felt alſo the Roll of *Engliſh* Lead', which he particularly covets. The lead has an almost magical presence – it has *almost* arrived on the island as the raw material of manufacturing society: it is an anticipation. Crusoe tries to tear pieces off with hatchets, and eventually is rewarded with 'near 100 Weight' – and that is the last we hear of it. With a later wreck he is more discriminating:

> I took a Fire Shovel and Tongs, which I wanted extremely; as alſo two little Braſs Kettles, a Copper Pot to make Chocolate, and a Gridiron.

From Sizzers to Sheat Lead to Chocolate Pots – here is the ship's manifest that offers itself up like a discarded shopping list of *stuff*: objects happened upon, come across, like stuff found up on a wall or down on a workshop table. Guy Fawkes's own lantern, for example, would appeal to Robinson Crusoe – or indeed to Richard Wentworth – not as a vitrinist anecdotal relic, but as an ingeniously designed lamp with a malleable beam:

> a cylindrical body of sheet iron with a candle-holder in the base and a hinged door with a translucent horn pane; a revolving inner cylinder with a louvered vent that can be rotated to shield the light….

## Trip

But Crusoe enumerates, he lists his possessions and confines them in serial structures: within fences and rooms, upon shelves, in pockets and in the hand – secure within the spaces and frames of ceiling, floor, and wall (spaces that have been so contested by twentieth-century artists). Such containers are fundamentally of the body: he is clothed and fabricates an umbrella to guard his immediate territory against inclement tropical weather. Here, limit gives identity, a limit secured and defined within belts and pouches, muskets and perspective glasses (telescopes). Such a drive towards the

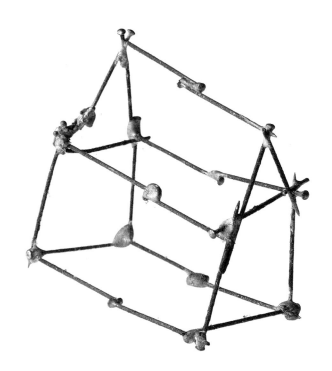

**28**

integrity of the list means that oddities, like 'two Shoes that were not Fellows', make an indelible impression on Crusoe. Odd shoes speak of fractured identity and broken being, rather than of liberation. Traces therefore become uncannily dynamic: the singular footprint suggests that another world is tripping up against his. The footprint simply doesn't fit the inventory of the island or the containment of the narrative. It is beyond the edge of explication, it marks the limit of Crusoe's analysis, Crusoe's interpretation, Crusoe's understanding.

## Chapter & Verse

Crusoe seeks succour in the big book of lists, the Bible: a popular book – translated into the holy vernacular, portable and manual, and provided with numbered verses for ready retrieval. The numbering of Biblical verses was a radical reconceptualisation of Scripture, encouraging its use as a proverbial repository – or as a list of magical spells to be summoned in adversity with a blind finger. This Bibliolatory is deployed by Crusoe in its most pragmatic and ecstatic form. The definitive phrase 'in a Word' recurs like a refrain throughout Crusoe's account. It is everywhere in his story: he is a man amazed and sublimely grateful that his excruciating tale can be expressed in words, 'in a Word', in *the* Word. The world thus becomes knowable and discoverable, graspable and fundamentally lexical. Robinson Crusoe is a lexicographer who possesses his island (always qualified as me/my/mine, as his 'eye' and himself, 'I') with words. He makes the broken, post-lapsarian text of the island legible, and, by marking time against a wooden post, he makes the island speak to him every day.

## Jack-in-the-Box

This enforced translation of the world into the word appears to be miraculous, and other miracles follow. Crusoe shakes husks out of a linen bag and in due course barley grows. His cut stakes forming a palisade grow into a hedge. In other words, he builds his environment, and is blind to the natural gestures of the island. He would build a turnpike and a string of inns if he could, imposing a consistency of surface and experience over the land.

Crusoe the great emigrant is also dead to the concept that things migrate, that meanings are fugitive(s) – such as his fence-becoming-hedge, his husks-becoming-wheat. He is not Joseph of Arimathea, whose flowering staff inspired Glastonbury, the first Christian church in England. Instead, Crusoe builds secular works: fortifications and look-outs. He is a genius of compartmentalisation. Everything must reside in a box,

35

on a shelf, in a pen, in a vitrine, in a cooking pot. He is in a perpetual state of war against nature, total war. Crusoe bakes clay and makes pots. Had he readymix concrete he would have doubtless embattled his whole island like the *Atlantikwall* – a lost outpost of another catastrophic empire. While it is difficult to see ramparts and bunkers as anything but symbolic, yet there are emergent meanings here, raised up by time like message bottles bobbing on the ocean, or drifting like mines across the sea. Old bits of war and colonialism are retrospective, but might be reconceptualised.

> War is at once a summary and a museum… fortifications aim not only to conserve power but also to conserve all combat techniques.[7]

Paul Virilio even compares bunkers with the avant-garde of art, 'Could war be prospective?'[8]

## Done

It is Daniel Defoe who becomes the artist of *Robinson Crusoe*: Defoe the projector who baked clay, Defoe the tireless prospector. Defoe puts Crusoe under the immense pressure of the future: to survive, to build and adapt and create, sometimes against the grain of his entrepreneurial acumen. Defoe writes laboriously, as laboriously as Crusoe constructs a shovel and 'a Thing like a Hodd' out of Ironwood: it takes four days to make the Shovel, the Hodd, and attempt in vain to make a Wheel-Barrow. Defoe also makes Crusoe make baskets, 'three large Pipkins, and two or three Pots'.

> If I wanted a Board, I had no other Way but to cut down a Tree, ſet it on an Edge before me, and hew it flat on either ſide with my Axe, till I had brought it to be thin as a Plank, and then dubb it ſmooth with my Adze. It is true, by this Method I could make but one Board out of a whole Tree…

As Richard Wentworth has remarked, this is another way of rethinking the island –

'*how flat, or long, or deep, must a tree be before it's a shelf?*' – and it is also a rethinking of time, which becomes strangely inconsequential in *Robinson Crusoe*. It takes the man 42 days to make a shelf – and yet, except to the diminishing calendar post that bears the scars of the past, time means nothing on the island. Crusoe expends 20 days in cutting down an enormous Cedar tree, a fortnight to trim the boughs off, a month to shape it, and three months to hollow it into a great canoe. The monster thus created is large enough to carry six-and-twenty men: 'had I gotten it into the Water, I make no queſtion but I ſhould have began the maddeſt Voyage, and the moſt unlikely to be perform'd,

SHELTER AT HOME

The New Government

# STEEL INDOOR 'TABLE' SHELTER

IS NOW AVAILABLE IN THIS DISTRICT : PARTICULARS FROM

that ever was undertaken'. But it lies a hundred yards from the water. Digging a canal, he reflects, will take at least a decade. 'I was oblig'd to let it lye where it was, as a *Memorandum* to teach me to be wifer next Time'. In this sense, the canoe does float – its being migrates from boat to moral lesson.

## Sandcastles

Despite Crusoe's insistence, the island is never simply a visible space: it is tracked and criss-crossed by invisible meanings. Lists, like Crusoe's journal, like the shipping forecast, speak most eloquently about what is left out. Gaps sing. The empty spaces are populated by cannibals that bark all too hungrily, for the world is bigger than mere co-ordinates, bigger than Crusoe, longer than his lists, longer than any list. Daniel Defoe is, however, tolerant of the irresponsibility of territory and of plotting. He is tolerant of the reprobate Crusoe (who fancies he is on the guestlist at the gate of heaven) because there is a demonic energy in material production, and he is tolerant of the new kinetic aspects of time and traffic across an island idyll. Defoe, then, is the real hero of *Robinson Crusoe*: an artist who will begin a list and not seek to finish it (there were two sequels to *Robinson Crusoe*…). If Crusoe's list-making presents itself as the absolute inventory of a handyman, the most useful tool in the world, it bores Defoe, who discards it like a superannuated shopping list. Defoe treats the activity of enumeration like a ladder (itself an ascending list of rungs) or an umbrella: apparently indispensable until its job is done, thereafter farcically cumbersome.

## Rule of Thumb

> The world in English is measured by the body – spans of hands and feet, a yard the length for nose to fingers at the end of an outstretched arm… This is the image of the body as implement, as moving in and through the environment in such a way that the material world is a physical extension of the needs and purposes of the body.[9]

The hand finds the handle, and turns the world into a swing of the arm. *Robinson Crusoe* is a novel of prostheses – like shovels and pouches, clothes and language – which manage the world surprisingly well. The island becomes a tracing of Crusoe's anatomy and of his precision with tools: whether the adze or the abc. Richard Wentworth might compare himself to Defoe managing Crusoe; comprehending the comprehension of the world, sorting it out.

In order to go from Tijuana to San Diego without crossing the Mexico/USA border, I will follow a perpendicular route away from the fence and circumnavigate the globe heading 67° SE, NE, and SE again until meeting my departure point.
The items generated by the journey will attest to the fulfillment of the task. The project will remain free and clear of all critical implications beyond the physical displacement of the artist.

**Para viajar de Tijuana a San Diego sin cruzar la frontera entre México y los Estados Unidos, tomaré una ruta perpendicular a la barda divisoria. Desplazándome 67° SE, luego hacia el NE y de nuevo hacia el SE, circunnavegaré la Tierra hasta llegar al punto de partida.**
**Los objetos generados por el viaje darán fe de la realización del proyecto, mismo que quedará libre de cualquier contenido crítico más allá del desplazamiento físico del artista.**

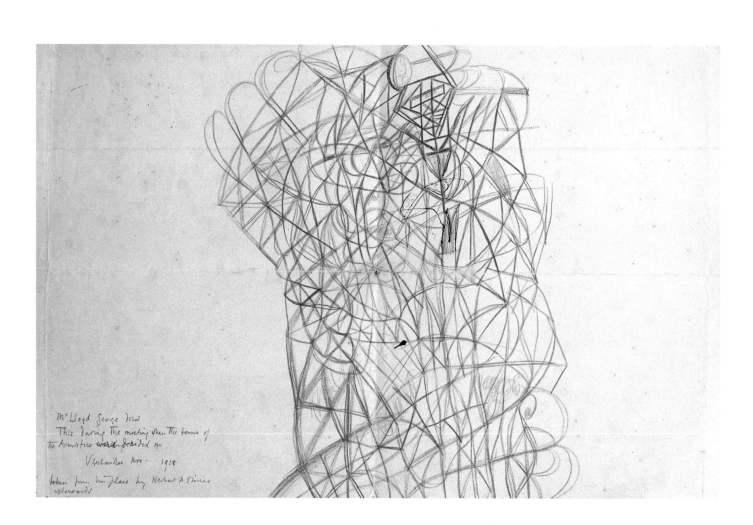

Mr Lloyd George drew
This during the meeting when the terms of
the Armistice were being decided on
Versailles Nov. 1918

taken from his place by Herbert A Olivier
afterwards

## Rifling

*I have always made the distinction between collect and acquire – one seeming more self-conscious. We acquire mannerisms and vocabulary and relationships, I think, more than we collect them. We are all acquisitive – I like the idea of rifling in Goethe's or Nietzsche's papers…*

Something is forgotten in acquisition. It is a less conscious activity than collecting. One loses oneself, for example, in relationships – or grubbing through the extant papers of a Goethe or a Nietzsche – and one forgets in order to re-form or re-member. Goethe left an epiphanic note in which he describes finding among his papers a sheet on which he called architecture 'frozen music'. Having forgotten or repressed one text, he reports it in another – which now survives. The idea returns like an insistent echo on the flimsiest material vehicle. Scrap paper, shopping lists, are the slightest physical shelters (in common with sand-filled bunkers, hutches, hats, or umbrellas), but they remain hedges against the future and against losing one's way. They are an extension of the body into time. Other rifling might rediscover forgetfulness. Among Nietzsche's papers is the fragment,

'I have forgotten my umbrella.'

Robinson Crusoe built himself an umbrella out of goatskins and in writing his memoir recalled or remembered it; Nietzsche only remembers he has forgotten.[10] The object has escaped into an elsewhere.

## Cancellanda

This forgetfulness is a proof of the materiality of objects. Objects are proofs: the proof of history and the mark of others, of disparate origin and of manufacture. And a *proof* in both senses: proof as verification and testimony to material history, and proof as a first draft or first impression – simply one narrative, one history, among many possibilities. Like the page-proofs of a book, objects join together to create material grammars of utility, which are allusive and full of potential. As Richard Wentworth puts it

*The coherence of some objects is formidable, the way all the tailored parts of a barrel add up to a whole, the myriad combinations which amount to 'car'…*

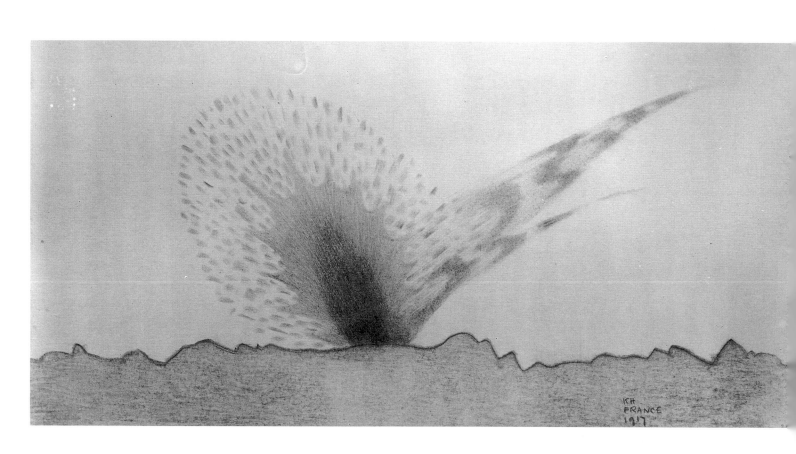

Yet still in all this functional confidence and craft, there is an elusive excess, the tale of the thing left hanging:

> ... *Set against this is the pathos of the lost key, or the blank, unswinging door whose key is missing – or the single shoe (often a child's) lying alone in the road...*

The object incorporates something outside of itself, it is supplemented by a quality that is neither part of the material construction of the object nor its history, but which bestows upon it an aura. In other words, the full definition of an object incorporates its future and a sense of its possible destinations, and without these an object is incomplete: it lacks the fulfilment of its destiny. Something from the future is always missing – and this lack is perhaps half-heard in synchronicity and through meaningful misrecognition.

## Was There Then

'*Where do certain realities lie?*'. One '*certain reality*' lies in the uncertainty of the flea market, a sort of gigantic skip, the last chance for commodity culture. The idea that an object can and will be extinguished might be alien to our material way of thinking, but at any flea market one can stand idly by as objects are liquidated. They bring stories and deathbed confessions; they might be Soviet and US fatigues thrown together in a sudden Cold War metaphor, or just '*something you grow up with*' like boxes of rusty nails, invisibly nostalgic. This debris is neither flotsam, nor jetsam: it is cast upon the waters, and sinks to the sea-bed. But being so close to immateriality these disappearing objects enjoy the embrace of impermanence. Almost wholly materially fulfilled, they are almost all there: replete because they face oblivion. Part of the essence of being, it appears, is impermanence.[11] So at the same time that objects become materially whole, they lose their future and their past. They become like anecdotes – secret, unprinted histories – 'all these nothings' as Sainte-Beuve described them.

*Thinking Aloud* is about pointing, then seizing and grasping, pulling the disappearing object out of the 'vast shipwreck of history',[12] then feeling its contours, the way it might fit the hand, charting the way it abuts other objects (goods, commodities, tools), and divining the haptic. '*Living in a ready-made landscape and putting it to work.*' How many ways can *that* be placed in the sifting jigsaw of the everyday: does it

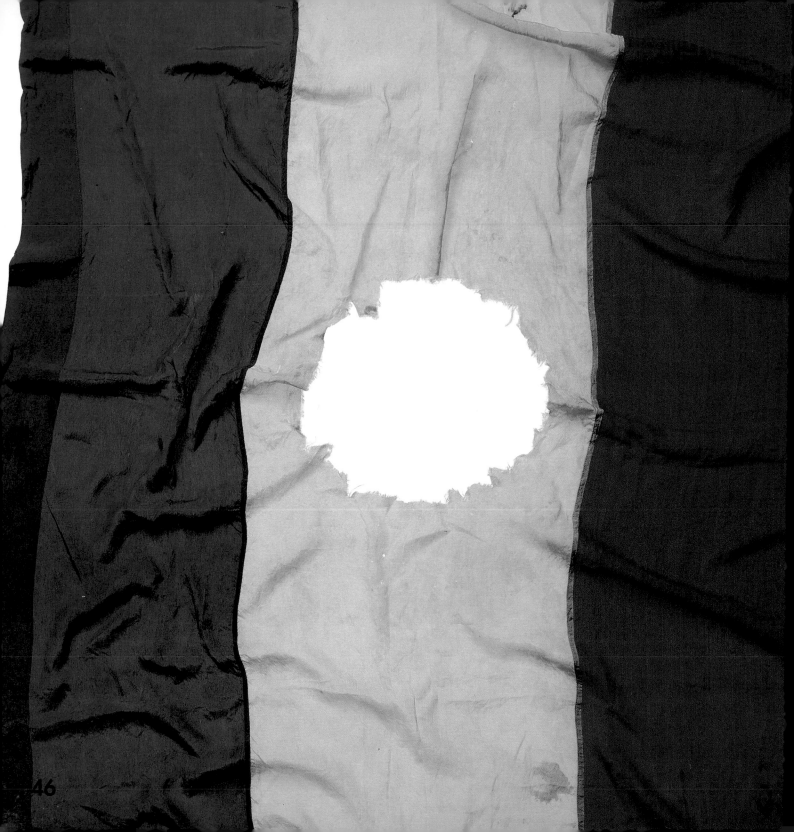

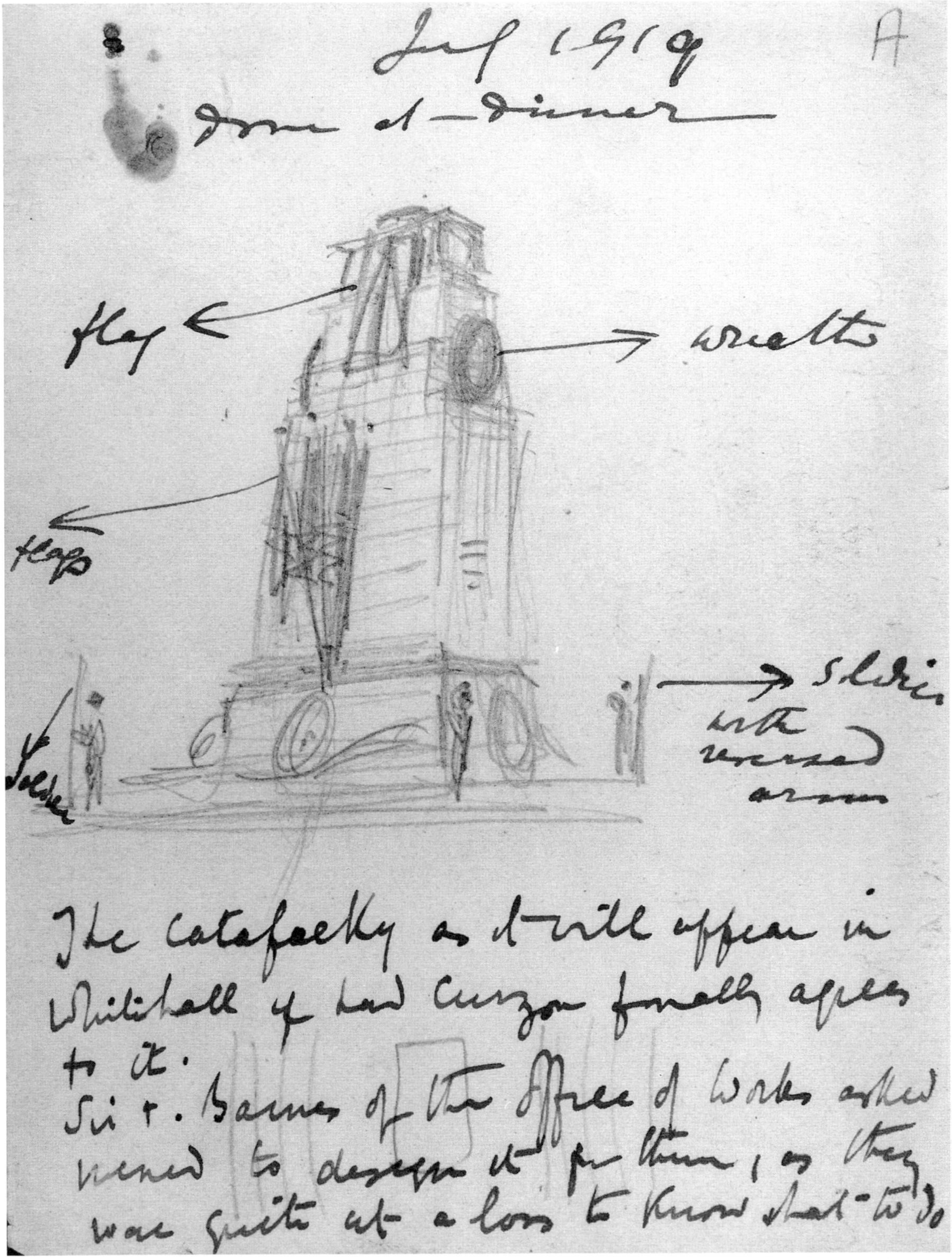

July 1919     A

Done at dinner

flag →

→ wreaths

← flags

→ soldiers
with
reversed
arms

Soldier

The catafalky as it will appear in
Whitehall if Lord Curzon finally agrees
to it.
Sir r. Barnes of the Office of Works asked
several to design it for them, as they
was quite at a loss to know what to do

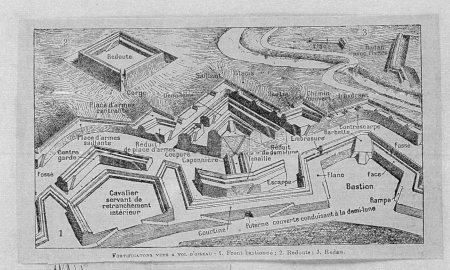

FORTIFICATIONS VUES A VOL D'OISEAU : 1. Front bastionné ; 2. Redoute ; 3. Redan.

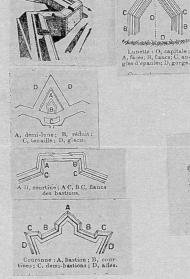

Bastion.

Lunette : O, capitale ; A, faces; B, flancs; C, angles d'épaules; D, gorge.

A, demi-lune ; B, réduit ; C, tenaille ; D, glacis.

A D, courtine ; A C, B C, flancs des bastions.

Couronne : A, bastion ; B, courtines ; C. demi-bastions ; D, ailes.

Coupe d'un fort d'arrêt moderne souterrain.

Gabion.

touch other tools or instruments, corners or the curl of fingers, ideas or experiments or experiences? '*It reminds me*', muses Richard Wentworth,

> *of how we hear of murders – the tent-peg, the half brick, the bottle, the kitchen scissors – all 'chosen' in the heat of the moment, and all perfect for the 'job'.*

## Ground

Shelters, like kitchen drawers and rubbish skips, are impositions of systematic order. They therefore help to construct knowledge (this is cutlery, that is rubbish), extending war into the domestic sphere by characterising a form of political control: Fascism – the minute regulation of every physical freedom. This form of warfare replots land, taking incipit territory and unrolling it, making the surface of the world explicit and obscenely legible like the most proactive school of cartography. Against these spatial politics of Fascism, the Last War (the Second World War) was in consequence fought by the Allies conceptually as well as physically, against the 'total war' of imperialism in which all space was prey to colonisation and exploitation. The Fascist war machine was driven by land acquisition. It was profoundly material: the sea and the air were simply adjuncts to the land – its peoples, its resources, its arcana.

Which returns us to the subversive armoury of the kitchen drawer or the transgressive art of the skip. Art exhibitions and performances totalise space as much as the art of war does. You arrive to be promptly and properly lost. You cannot locate yourself; but you really do know where you are. No-one arrives here by accident: you are in an art gallery (and, like train stations, they are all pretty much the same).

> *There is an implicit act of intention in going to an art gallery: a physical organisational effort. This act of will, like picking up a book, is somehow at odds with the necessity to then relax into the fictions which the space proposes – it is an experiential oxymoron. You have to go with this other condition, or leave…*

This *other condition* is the pretence of unknowing, knowingly mistaking the gallery for some fabulously elegant wrecker's yard… An art gallery, then, is some attitude you inhabit, a form of power-dressing (like Crusoe's civilizing clothes), and to escape this condition one must make space fluid and dynamic in criss-crossing trajectories. The tactical response to Fascism was to 'dematerialize' the ground, and Allied armies made their weapons mobile and autonomous – all-terrain, amphibious hybrid equipment.[13] Likewise, the response to total art exhibitions is to show more than mere art.

## Figure

The Nazi war machine codified violence as its written set of rules for political land management, rules that the Allies repeatedly and instinctively broke with Q-Ships, counter-intelligence, and inflatable tanks. Richard Wentworth tells a story of a German interviewer, who suggested to the Allied top brass that they hadn't played the game fairly: '*you were always pretending… you would always be making fake things suggesting you would be turning up somewhere where you weren't and then not doing it…*'. The British war effort was the greatest work of fiction of the twentieth century: full of dummies and decoys (and their opposite – camouflage), the work of espionage and escapes and terrorist funding and disinformation and lies.[14]

## Back to the Front

The military, then, is a set of propositions. It proposes new technologies (the main reason for going into space was military strategy) and the most familiar of everyday technologies, from tinned food to photography to concrete, from the Internet to 747s to the Ordnance Survey – '*all these things which are embedded in our daily activity*' – tend to be financed and pushed forward by the military. The secret of such advances is that they are oddly regressive. In reaching the tactical sphere of outer space, what was discovered was not the moon but, upon looking back, a new vision of the earth: a new, swirling, orbital photograph of the globe. Exploration is not simply progressive, it also hearkens back, nostalgically, and relocates you and your point of presumed origin. Crusoe on his island writes an epic of applied knowledge in which the world is made all-too legible: a worldly autobiography, a new edition of the world. For writing and especially publishing is a form of hedging, a physical enclosure of non-visual spaces and senses; it too regulates and standardises. Printing technology enabled the standardisation of the Book of Prayer and consequently the standardisation of the day and the year. Print created spelling conformity and deviation, interior space, and inner consciousness, and the medium of domestic lore changed from the oral tradition to almanacs and herbals, and thence to household codes and directions for social conduct.

## Different Class

The point is to notice and mobilise different sorts of difference. There are other ways of reading, enumerating, or handling things. Tools are different, and actions differ. Marcel Mauss noticed during the Great War that French and English soldiers used hoes differently: that if the English tend to push their forks and spades, the

49

(continued from page 21)

Hello, Waddington Galleries.

No, you have the wrong number.

OK.

[click]  [click]

☎ ☎

[Ringing tone]  [Ringing tone]
Antony D'Offay

Good afternoon, Waddington Galleries.

Hello?
Sorry, this is the Antony D'Offay gallery.

No, no, it's not.

No, this is ... I ... I ... just ... I don't know how
we're being connected here.

Oh right. OK. (laughs)

OK?  Bye bye.
[click]  [click]

☎ ☎

[Ringing tone]  [Ringing tone]
Antony D'Offay.

(Pause) Hello?

Yes?

Were you answering an incoming call?

Excuse me? ... Yes ... yes, we were.

Er, this is Waddington Galleries ... I was ...

I think they're playing around with the, um ...
with the exchange or something, doing some ...

No, there is something very peculiar going on,
and I think Mr Waddington has already
complained about it, because what is curious, it
appears to be galleries who get ...

Yes.

That's absolutely right. I ... I was just saying to
someone it happened to me on Friday with
Annely Juda ... I don't really know what's going
on ...

And what's more wei ... yes ... We have had it
happening with, um, I mean there is something
funny going on, we've had it happening with
Nicholas Logsdail at the ... Lisson, which is no
way even in the same vicinity ...

Yes.

Yearh, yuh, I don't know what to say.

Um, well I'm just going to note it down, it ...
because I think the more one knows precisely ...
so, OK ... we ...

Hmm.
Well I've been on to the exchange here ... um

Yes, and I'll find out who we've got on to
because I know ... a ... something was being done
at the end of last week.

Yes, OK (laughs)
Thank you, bye bye.  OK. Thank you. (laughs) bye.
[click]  [click]

☎ ☎

[Ringing tone]  [Ringing tone]
Hello, Interim Art.

Hello, Karsten Schubert gallery.

(laughs) There's something really weird going on
... um, sorry, I'm calling from Maureen's.

Oh.

E ... every now and then, our phone rings
(laughs) I pick it up and the it starts ringing and
then (laughing) another gallery picks up at the
other end.

We ... we had exactly the same problem with
Laure Genillard, it's so weird.

Well no I ... I've now had Annely Juda and
Antony Reynolds and we're obviously moving
further afield than Dering Street.

That is so ... so weird, I don't understand it at all.

Noo ... (laughs) I'm glad you've got the same
problem (laughing) I don't know what it is.  (laughs)
OK, well, there we are.

OK, well, (laughing) nice to talk to you anyway.
Bye.  Bye.
[click]  [click]

☎ ☎

[Ringing tone]  [Ringing tone]
Salama-Caro Gallery.
(Pause) Hello? (Pause)

Victoria Miro Gallery.  [click]

(background noise)
Hello?
(Pause) Hello?
[click]

☎ ☎

[Ringing tone]  [Ringing tone]
Morning, Antony Reynolds.  Annely Juda Fine Art.
(Pause) Hello?

Hello?

(Pause) Can I help you?

(Pause) I'm sorry, our phone just rang.

Sorry?

Sorry, who's calling?

This is Annely Juda Fine Art.

(Pause) Oh ... err ... seems to be some problem ...
our phone just rang.  Oh. (laughs) wh ... where are you? (Pause) I'm
through a crossed line.

Ye ... es ...  OK then, cause our phone just rang, so I just
picked it up, alright then.

OK then, thank you.

Bye.  OK, bye.
[click]  [click]

☎ ☎

[Ringing tone]  [Ringing tone]
Antony D'Offay.
(background voices)
(Pause) Hello?
(Pause) Hello?

Hello, Lisson Gallery.

Oh ... (talking to someone else) hey ... it's
happened now

Hello?

Hello.

Yes, this is ... Hello?

Yes, hello, this is the Antony D'Offay gallery ...
um ...

N ... no ... oh, is it?

Yes, we just um, I just (laughs) picked up a line
that was ringing , and I got you.

Right.

I ... is this the Lisson Gallery?

Yes it is. We ...we just did the same thing.

W ... well so where exactly are you, North West
One is it?

Yes it is.

So li ... we've just got British Telecom in actually
(background voices), incidentally, and we ...
we're reporting this sort of weird sort of crossed
line situation that's occurring (laughing) for
about four days , it's sort of Waddington's, no
one else ...  I know, well we need to do the same, it happens
Hmm ... ... so it's quite weird because we're not even in
Yup ... the same area.

Exactly, and ...it happens really often.

Yes ... I ... I'll report it to British Telecom also.
Yeah ... can I have your number actually?  It ...
Your phone number.  er ... our phone number is seven two four, two
seven three nine.

Yuh, ... two seven three nine, thank you.

Bye.  OK? bye.
[click]  [click]

☎ ☎

[Ringing tone]  [Ringing tone]
Good morning, Waddington Galleries.

Hello, Lisson Gallery.

(Pause) Sorry?

Hello, Lisson Gallery.

Um ... I'm sorry, I just picked the phone up ... um,
I got an incoming call for Waddington's.

Oh my god, I can't believe this is happening.

Have you told ... the, um ...

Yeah, we've told them and told them and told
them.
Yearh, we had Telecom in again this morning.  This is crazy.

I know, cause we've had sort of various other
galleries on the phone as well.

(continued inside back cover)

Mediterraneans pull their mattocks and picks. And Eugène Gaspard Marin devoted himself to producing a taxonomy of such application.[15]

Gaspard Marin (1883–1969) was a Belgian anarchist, an anthropologist whose idiosyncratic works fill a chamber of the Museum of Mankind – and conceivably an outsider artist: '*someone who had heard of Marcel Broodthaers but misunderstood the project*'. He was little known in his lifetime and is almost completely forgotten today, but his work is recognisably thinking aloud. Marin set himself the extreme modernist task of supreme classification, aiming to convert thought into completely negotiable and universal space (he was a keen advocate of Esperanto). He collected pictures and descriptions of prostheses (like umbrellas, barrels, and weapons) or architecture (like fences and palisades), often cutting these received images from greetings cards, stamps, and photos, retrieving them from evanescent ephemera, pasting them into pocket-sized books...

## Half a Mo

Marin was a formalist: he broke objects or activities into constituent parts, each of which was assigned a letter and number. (He is not unlike Funes the Memorious, who invented a new system of numbering: '... In place of five hundred, he would say *nine*...'.[16]) Marin considered his most important work to be on time-reckoning, which was classified by geographical area, and thence into cycles, the division of days, series of days, definitions of month and year, a table on how the year was organised, and series of years. He also noted festival days and devices for recording time, and each component was then translated into a bewildering series of letters, numbers, and symbols. Finally, this information was amalgamated and classified according to intervals of time, from the smallest to the largest: from the 'twinkling of an eye' or smoking a pipe, to years and aeons.

## Receipt

Marin's work is based purely on function, and there is a pleasing readiness about the whole project. In his collection of firelighters, for example, he includes (from Germany) a drawing of an 'Old chisel having served as a fire-steel'. But what is striking about Marin's use of this firelighter is his brilliant Crusoe-like clarity of perception. Marin already knows what he is going to see. His collection confirms knowledge and secures

52

53

55

identity in a custom-built utopia, as part of a total, supposedly liberating system. Here is his recipe code for mashed potatoes:

*sol K (or B) Ų + b + mus + h + l*
[literal translation: potatoes bake (or boil) pass through sieve add butter add nutmeg add salt add milk]

Marin's project is, as Richard Wentworth puts it, *'the legitimation of reverie'*.

## Ampersand

Richard Wentworth is not Gaspard Marin any more than he is Robinson Crusoe, but all three are sorters and sifters, and sorting and sifting is above all the activity of the individual artist. The residue of their sorting becomes another object in the canon of objects, which for Crusoe and Marin can run on interminably. But Richard Wentworth's art, his exhibition-making and collecting and acquiring, creates escape routes for objects. It is heterotopian (many-futured):

in such a state, things are 'laid', 'placed', 'arranged' in sites so very different from one another that it is impossible to find a place of residence for them, to define a *common locus* beneath them all...[17]

Heterotopias unhinge common order and common sense, question the exercises of civilising and civilisation, and contest the very possibility of grammar. Propagation is not by families and primogeniture, but 'by epidemic, by contagion'.[18] These are revolutionary lists: redefinition in the multitude, in bands and packs and rhizomic spread, in the endemic, in heterogeneity. How do we name the objects that arise into this new disorder. Art? And where do we put them? They don't fit into the space in which they are shown. Where will *thinking aloud* begin, or end? Is any of this *thinking allowed*?

Notes

1  I am extremely grateful to Richard Wentworth for several discussions, interviews, and faxes that have contributed so much to this essay that we have forgotten who said or wrote what. I am also deeply indebted to Roger Malbert and Marina Warner for practical help and sage advice.

2  Jorge Luis Borges, in *Dreamtigers* (London: Souvenir Press, 1973), gives as his source Suarez Miranda: *Viajes de Varones Prudentes*, Book Four, Chapter XLV, Lérida, 1658 (90).

3  Quoted by Michel Foucault, *The Order of Things: An Archaeology of the Human Sciences* (London: Routledge, 1970), xvi.

4  Jorge Luis Borges, 'The Analytical Language of John Wilkins', *Other Inquisitions* (Austin: University of Texas Press, 1964), quoted by Foucault, xv.

5  Foucault, 59.

6  See Valentine Cunningham, *In the Reading Gaol: Postmodernity, Texts, and History* (Oxford, UK & Cambridge, USA: Blackwell, 1994), 161–2; Susan Stewart, *On Longing: Narratives of the Miniature, the Gigantic, the Souvenir, the Collection* (Durham & London: Duke University Press, 1993), 15–16; and Hubert Damisch 'Robinsonnades I & II', tr. Rosalind Krauss, *October* 85 (Summer 1998), 19–40. All quotations are taken from the Norton edition of *Robinson Crusoe*, ed. Michael Shinagel (New York & London: W. W. Norton & Co., 1975).

7  Paul Virilio, *Bunker Archeology*, tr. George Collins (New York: Princeton Architectural Press, 1994), 27.

8  Virilio, 14.

9  Stewart, 101–2.

10  Jacques Derrida, *Spurs: Nietzsche's Styles*, tr. B. Harlow (Chicago: University of Chicago Press, 1979), 123–43.

11  Martin Johnston, 'Games With Infinity', *Jacket Magazine* 1 (http://www.jacket.zip.com.au/jacket01/mj-borges.html).

12  Francis Bacon, *Dignity and Advancement of Learning*, ed. Spedding, Ellis, & Heath (London: Longman, 1858), iv. 303.

13  Virilio, 41.

14  See, for example, Jean Baudrillard, *The Gulf War Did Not Take Place*, tr. Paul Patton (Sydney: Power Publications, 1995).

15  Gaspard Marin has been only recently rediscovered. My information on him is based on Sara Pimpaneau's excellent MA Dissertation, 'The Marin Collection: A Description and Analysis of Eugène Gaspard Marin's Methodology' (London, 1997), and other unpublished essays. My thanks to her.

16  Jorge Luis Borges, 'Funes the Memorious', *Labyrinths*, tr. James E. Irby (Harmondsworth: Penguin, 1970), 93.

17  Foucault, xviii.

18  Gilles Deleuze and Félix Guattari, *A Thousand Plateaus: Capitalism and Schizophrenia*, tr. Brian Massumi (London: Athlone Press, 1988), 241.

# Illustrations

Objects in the exhibition illustrated in this book

**1** Cardboard box of remaindered toy dinosaurs
Photo: Mike Parsons

**2** MacDonald Gill
Map of the Underground Railways of London, 1923
printed paper
37.2 × 45.4 cm
London Transport Museum
© London Transport Museum

**3** Frank O. Gehry
Sketch of Weatherhead School of Management at Case Western Reserve University
ink on paper
22.9 × 30.5 cm
Frank O. Gehry & Associates
© Frank O. Gehry & Associates 1998

**4** David Shrigley
Ignore this Building, 1998
c-print
39 × 49 cm
Courtesy of the artist and Stephen Friedman Gallery
© the artist 1998

**5** Patrick Caulfield
Sculpture in a Landscape, 1966
oil on board
121.9 × 213.3 cm
Arts Council Collection, Hayward Gallery, London
© the artist 1998

**6** Brassaï
Sculpture involontaire: Billet d'autobus roulé ('Symmetrically' rolled bus ticket, very rare form of morphologic automatism with evident beginnings of stereotypism), c.1932
photograph
17 × 24 cm
Courtesy of Gilberte Brassaï
© copyright Gilberte Brassaï – all rights reserved

**7** Frank O. Gehry
Design process model of the Weatherhead School of Management at Case Western Reserve University, 30 October 1997
brown paper, silver paper, wood, plastic, foam core structure and base
45.7 × 66 × 81.3 cm
Frank O. Gehry & Associates
© Frank O. Gehry & Associates 1998

**8** Sir Joseph Paxton
First sketches for The Great Exhibition Building of 1851, 1850
ink on blotting paper
39 × 28 cm
The Victoria and Albert Museum

**9** Gary Hume
Box of drawings on A4-sized acetate for projecting and colouring in
Collection of the artist
© the artist 1998

**10** Diana – The People's Princess – 1961–1997, November 1997
Designed, produced and published by Compulsion Creative Concepts Limited
41 × 51 cm
Photo: Mike Parsons

**11** Anya Gallaccio
Broken English August '91, 1997
screenprint
68 × 88.5 cm
Collection Joe and Felix Wentworth
© the artist 1998

**12** Walker Evans
Household supply store, Bethlehem PA, November 1935
photograph
20.3 × 25.4 cm
Library of Congress, Washington D.C.

**13** Standard Kilogram, copy with glass cover, 1889
platinum-10% iridium, glass
4 × 4 cm
The National Physical Laboratory
© Crown Copyright 1989.
Reproduced by permission of the Controller of HMSO

**14** Walker Evans
Vacuum cleaner factory, Arthur Dale Projects, Reedsville, West Virginia, July 1935
photograph
20.3 × 25.4 cm
Library of Congress, Washington D.C.

**15** Drawings for patent of flip-top cigarette packet, 1939
British Patent 507,998

**16** Tania Kovats
Vera, 1997
plaster, flocking, steel bracket
33 × 210 × 22 cm
Asprey Jacques, London
© the artist 1998

**17** Mariele Neudecker
Never Eat Shredded Wheat (Memory Maps), 1996
acrylic and felt pen on paper
9 parts, each 88 × 112 cm
Arts Council Collection, Hayward Gallery, London
© the artist 1998

**18** Gaspard Marin (1883–1969)
Notebook entitled 'Algebre' (letters in form of branches) containing his notes on world history and loose-leaf maps. Pl. 308 with stamps from Esztergom
19 × 13 cm
The British Museum Department of Ethnography Library
© British Museum

**19** Patrick Keiller
Robinson in Space: schematic diagram of itinerary
ink drawing on acetate overlaid on map
Courtesy of the artist

**20** War Office
Section of the D-Day Briefing Model for Normandy Landings, 1944
wooden frame with stretched fabric, paint
5.1 × 61 × 61 cm
Imperial War Museum, London

**21** Julian Opie
Landscape?, 1997
vinyl and aluminium
240 × 336 × 10 cm
Courtesy of Lisson Gallery, London
© the artist 1998

**22** John Riddy
Normandy, 1995
photograph
38 × 48 cm
Courtesy of Frith Street Gallery, London
© the artist 1998

**23** Walker Evans
Farm near Jackson, Mississippi, March 1936
photograph
20.3 × 25.4 cm
Library of Congress, Washington D.C.

**24** BBC Shipping-Map for Weather Bulletins
The Met. Office
Courtesy of The Met. Office

**25** Modern illustration of historical progression of standard lengths measurement from the Henry VIII yard to a modern end standard
The National Physical Laboratory
© Crown Copyright 1989.
Reproduced by permission of the Controller of HMSO

**26** Gaspard Marin (1883–1969)
Page with illustrations of hooks, from a folder containing loose pages with collages of illustrations taken from a Larousse dictionary. Several folders containing these pages are held together in the original binding of the 'Handbook to the Ethnological Collection' of the British Museum
22 × 14 cm
The British Museum Department of Ethnography Library
© British Museum

**27** Lucy Gunning
Climbing Round My Room, 1993
video
running time: 7½ minutes
Arts Council Collection, Hayward Gallery, London
© the artist 1998

**28** Pin house – child's metalwork experiment, 1990
Photo: Mike Parsons

**29** Andreas Gursky
Atlanta, 1996
c-print
186 × 260 cm
The Saatchi Gallery, London

**30** Walker Evans
House construction, Arthur Dale Project, Reedsville, West Virginia, June 1935
photograph
20.3 × 25.4 cm
Library of Congress, Washington D.C.

**31** Steve Johnson
Charm no. 9 (passport), 1996
bronze
10 × 14.5 × 2 cm
Collection of Delfina Entrecanales
© the artist 1998
Photo: Martyn Evans

**32** Map made into summer skirt and top, India, WWII
silk
top 26.7 × 55.9 cm;
skirt 69.9 × 121.9 cm
Imperial War Museum, London

**33** Dynamite (In Anticipation of an Explosion)
wood
Courtesy of Cornelia Parker
Photo: Mike Parsons

**34** Skateboard with camouflage grip tape
Courtesy of Leo Bessant and Felix Wentworth
Photo: Mike Parsons

**35** Percyval Tudor-Hart
Camouflaged sniper's gloves, 1917
matt oil-based paints on cotton
25.5 × 12.5 cm
Imperial War Museum, London
© Estate of Percyval Tudor-Hart 1998

**36** Architect's tree rubber stamp, one of five
obsolete drafting aid
Photo: Mike Parsons

**37** Tim Head
State of the Art, 1984
colour photograph
183 × 274 cm
Arts Council Collection, Hayward Gallery, London
© the artist 1998

**38** Shelter At Home, WWII
lithograph on paper
75.5 × 50.1 cm
Imperial War Museum, London

**39** Walker Evans
Photographer's window of penny portraits, Birmingham, Alabama, March 1936
photograph
20.3 × 25.4 cm
Library of Congress, Washington D.C.

**40** Harry Burton
Tutankhamun's tomb during excavation: Bow Box 80 with the lid removed
photograph
24.6 × 18.7 cm
The Griffith Institute, Ashmolean Museum, Oxford

**41** Francis Alÿs
'The loop' (a route around the globe following the Pacific Route, June 1 to July 5, 1997), postcard souvenir of the journey
2 postcards
each 10.3 × 14.9 cm
Courtesy of the artist
© the artist 1998

**42** Lloyd George
Drawing with inscription: 'Mr Lloyd George drew this during the meeting when the Terms of the Armistice were decided on. Versailles Nov 1918. Taken from his place by Herbert A. Olivier'. Olivier was an official war artist at Versailles, 1918
red pencil and ink on blotting paper
Imperial War Museum, London

**43** Keith Henderson
Study of a Shell-Burst, France, 1917
charcoal on paper
17.7 × 32.3 cm
Imperial War Museum, London
Courtesy of Imperial War Museum London

**44** Model of explosion, part of toy soldier set, German, 1930–39
plaster composition
George Hardie
Photo: Mike Parsons

**45** Ceal Floyer
Garbage Bag, 1996
black bin liner, twist tie, air
60 × 50 × 50 cm
Courtesy of Lisson Gallery, London
© the artist 1998

**46** Romanian banner with emblem of the former Socialist Republic of Romania removed by participant in the revolution of December 1989
Courtesy of Peasants' Museum, Bucharest
Photo: Mike Parsons

**47** Sir Edwin L. Lutyens
The Cenotaph (3), July 1919
pencil, colour pencil, ink
12.5 × 9.3 cm
Imperial War Museum, London

**8** Gaspard Marin (1883–1969)
?age with illustrations of different
?inds of fortifications from a folder
?ontaining loose pages with
?ollages of illustrations taken
?om a Larousse dictionary. Several
?olders containing these pages are
?eld together in the original binding
?f the 'Handbook to the Ethnological
?ollection' of the British Museum
?2 × 14 cm
?he British Museum Department
?f Ethnography Library
? British Museum

**9** Right Angle Bird's Nest
?hoto: Mike Parsons

**0** Angus Fairhurst
?allery Connections, 1991
?assette tape and Walkman with
?ped transcript
?ourtesy of the artist and Sadie
?les HQ
?etail from project for *Frieze*, Issue 0,
?991: © Angus Fairhurst 1998

**1** Ratonera (Spanish mousetrap)
?hoto: Mike Parsons

**2** Bernd and Hilla Becher
?al Washing Plant, Tower Colliery,
?rwaun, South Wales
?hotograph
?ll & Jack Wendler, London

**3** Bernd and Hilla Becher
?al Washing Plant, Ferndale
?olliery, Rhondda Valley, South
?ales, 1975
?otograph
?ll & Jack Wendler, London

? Harry Burton
?tankhamun's tomb during exca-
?tion: model oars in situ along the
?rth wall of the burial chamber
?otograph
?.8 × 24.9 cm
?e Griffith Institute, Ashmolean
?useum, Oxford

? Rachel Whiteread
?ntitled, 1993
?nze
?3 × 20.3 × 6.3 cm
?vate collection, London
?the artist 1998 – courtesy Jay
?oling/White Cube, London

?nt cover:
?zard warning sign
?nted steel
?oto: Mike Parsons

?ck cover:
?droit fréquenté par des enfants'
?nch street sign
?oto: Mike Parsons

# Inventory

Objects in the exhibition not
illustrated in this book

'A la Découverte de L'Espace'
20 plastic moulded astronauts with
United States flag in a vinyl bag
Made in China

Air Ministry Survey of Heathrow,
1943
76 × 99 cm
British Airport Authority

Alarm rattle (air raid protection),
1939
beech

Alarm rattle (bird scarer), 1850–1950
ash, metal
Birmingham Museums & Art Gallery

All Clear
photolithograph on paper
28.6 × 54 cm
Imperial War Museum, London

Artificial limbs: The Collins Hand
black and white archive film
on video
Courtesy of Steeper Ltd

Henry C. Beck
Original sketch for the London
Underground Railways Map, 1931
pencil and coloured inks on
squared paper
19 × 24.5 cm
The Victoria and Albert Museum

Body bag
The Hammersmith Hospitals,
NHS Trust

Bowl, 17th century
wood
Birmingham Museums & Art Gallery

Braille typewriter with alphabet
and braille translations
wood, metal and paper
29 × 31 cm
Courtesy of Helen Luckett

Brick mould (Press D. E Box & Plate)
cast iron
45 × 29 × 13 cm
Baggeridge Brick plc

Marcel Broodthaers
Les Animaux de la Ferme, 1974
2 colour prints
82 × 60.3 cm
Nell & Jack Wendler, London

Stanley Brouwn
This Way Brouwn
(Weteringschans) [1], 1968
black ballpoint pen on paper
124.4 × 156.8 cm
Stedelijk Museum Amsterdam

Stanley Brouwn
This Way Brouwn
(Weteringschans) [2], 1968
black ballpoint pen on paper
125 × 156.7 cm
Stedelijk Museum Amsterdam

Stanley Brouwn
This Way Brouwn
(Weteringschans) [3], 1969
black ballpoint pen on paper
110.2 × 156.5 cm
Stedelijk Museum Amsterdam

Stanley Brouwn
This Way Brouwn
(Weteringschans) [4], 1969
black ballpoint pen on paper
125 × 156.8 cm
Stedelijk Museum Amsterdam

Stanley Brouwn
This Way Brouwn
(Weteringschans) [5], 1969
black ballpoint pen on paper
121.6 × 156.5 cm
Stedelijk Museum Amsterdam

Ordo Amoris Cabinet (Francis
Acea and Diango Hernández)
Inventory, 1998
mixed media
dimensions variable
Collection of the artists

3 cheese-shaped wooden bowls
for throwing in a game rather like
skittles
lignum vitae
Birmingham Museums & Art Gallery

Chinese school globe, 1983
12 laminated and varnished paper
sections
15 cm diameter

Winston Churchill
Seascape, 1920s
oil on canvas
51 × 61 cm
Government Art Collection

Hannah Collins
BED, 1996
silver gelatin print mounted on
cotton
193 × 259 cm
Collection of the artist

The Collins prosthetic hand, c.1966
perspex and nylon cable
Courtesy of Steeper Ltd

Joan V. Connew
Blackout, 1942
oil on canvas
50.8 × 76.2 cm
Imperial War Museum, London

5 convex stainless-steel security
mirrors
London Underground, Northern
Line

Miles Coolidge
Safetyville, Commercial Building,
Capitol High Rises, 1994
c-print
76.2 × 96.5 cm
Casey Kaplan Gallery, New York
and Victoria Miro Gallery, London

Miles Coolidge
Safetyville, Industrial Buildings, 1994
c-print
76.2 × 99.1 cm
Casey Kaplan Gallery, New York
and Victoria Miro Gallery, London

Miles Coolidge
Safetyville, Store Front Denny's,
1994
c-print
76.2 × 99.1 cm
Casey Kaplan Gallery, New York
and Victoria Miro Gallery, London

'Danger Pièges' sign
French agricultural

Richard Deacon
Art For Other People, No. 44, 1997
wood and epoxy resin
18 × 32 × 17 cm
Collection Elisabeth McCrae

Deflated globe, 1980s
vinyl
Made in Taiwan

Durex condom mould
glass former
London International plc

James Dyson
Dyson prototype, 1978
adjusted vacuum cleaner
Courtesy of James Dyson

Electrical fitment (light fitting),
1900–30
wood, brass, steel
Birmingham Museums & Art Gallery

Electrical fitment (plug), c.1925–35
wood, brass
Birmingham Museums & Art Gallery

Walker Evans
Sharecropper's grave, Hale
County, Alabama, 1935
photograph
20.3 × 25.4 cm
Library of Congress,
Washington D.C.

Walker Evans
Family snapshots on wall of room
in Frank Tengle's home, Hale
County, Alabama, 1936
photograph
20.3 × 25.4 cm
Library of Congress,
Washington D.C.

Walker Evans
Soil erosion near Jackson,
Mississippi, March 1936
photograph
20.3 × 25.4 cm
Library of Congress,
Washington D.C.

Walker Evans
Soil erosion near Jackson,
Mississippi, March 1936
photograph
20.3 × 25.4 cm
Library of Congress,
Washington D.C.

Walker Evans
Soil erosion near Jackson,
Mississippi, March 1936
photograph
20.3 × 25.4 cm
Library of Congress,
Washington D.C.

Walker Evans
Soil erosion near Jackson,
Mississippi, March 1936
photograph
20.3 × 25.4 cm
Library of Congress,
Washington D.C.

Walker Evans
Soil erosion near Jackson,
Mississippi, March 1936
photograph
20.3 × 25.4 cm
Library of Congress,
Washington D.C.

Walker Evans
Soil erosion near Jackson,
Mississippi, March 1936
photograph
20.3 × 25.4 cm
Library of Congress,
Washington D.C.

Walker Evans
Soil erosion, Mississippi, March
1936
photograph
20.3 × 25.4 cm
Library of Congress,
Washington D.C.

Walker Evans
Soil erosion, vicinity of Edwards,
Mississippi, March 1936
photograph
20.3 × 25.4 cm
Library of Congress,
Washington D.C.

Finger protector / dibber?, 1900–25
wood
Birmingham Museums & Art Gallery

Joel Fisher
Letters (Double Alphabet), 1979–81
pencil and conté crayon on
handmade paper
46 × 572 cm
Arts Council Collection, Hayward
Gallery, London

Barry Flanagan
Elephant, 1981
bronze
50 × 41.5 × 24.1 cm
The artist, courtesy Waddington
Galleries, London

Stefan Gec
Buoy, 1996
1:10 scale maquette, mixed media
58 cm high
Courtesy of The Laboratory at the
Ruskin School of Drawing and
Fine Art, University of Oxford

Gilbert & George
Battle: A Postcard Sculpture, 1980
postcards on board
66 × 127 cm
Imperial War Museum, London

Gilbert & George
Victory March: A Postcard
Sculpture, 1980
postcards on board
66 × 127 cm
Imperial War Museum, London

6 glovo darning oggs in box,
19th century
boxwood, cardboard, glass, paper,
wool
Birmingham Museums & Art Gallery

Gold ingot mould
cast iron
Johnson Matthey Bullion Refinery

Antony Gormley
Five Fishes, 1982
lead
7 × 70 × 200 cm
Arts Council Collection, Hayward Gallery, London

Keith Henderson
Study of a Shell-Burst, France, 1917
charcoal on paper
28.5 × 19 cm
Imperial War Museum, London

Interlocking alphabet set, 1875–1950
sycamore
Birmingham Museums & Art Gallery

Sir Alec Issigonis
Sketch design for the Mini showing subframe and suspension details, 1956
felt-tipped pen on paper
25.4 × 33.1 cm
The Victoria and Albert Museum

Jig-saw puzzle in box
Labelled on lid 'The World dissected on the best principles for teaching geography', 1785–95
mahogany, paper, metal
Birmingham Museums & Art Gallery

Patrick Keiller
Robinson in Space: list of press cuttings compiled in chronological order, then sorted by location on itinerary
Courtesy of the artist

Alec Knight
Soldier Guarding an Aerodrome, 1940–43?
pencil, conté and wash on paper
25.4 × 20.3 cm
Imperial War Museum, London

Sir Edwin L. Lutyens
The Cenotaph (2), July 1919
pencil, colour pencil, ink
25.4 × 20.5 cm
Imperial War Museum, London

Sir Edwin L. Lutyens
The Cenotaph (4), July 1919
pencil, colour pencil, ink
9.3 × 12.5 cm
Imperial War Museum, London

Sir Edwin L. Lutyens
The Cenotaph (5), July 1919
pencil, colour pencil, ink
19.3 × 12.5 cm
Imperial War Museum, London

Map drawn by Dutch prisoner of war in Japanese Camp, showing progress of troop advances on the Russian front, WWII
paper
42 × 35.5 cm
Imperial War Museum, London

Gaspard Marin (1883–1969)
Loose pages with notes on Egyptian culture and history held in a thick green folder entitled 'Egypt'
18 × 22 cm
The British Museum Department of Ethnography Library

Gaspard Marin (1883–1969)
Loose pages with notes on games and their classification held in a thick beige card folder
21 × 14 cm
The British Museum Department of Ethnography Library

Gaspard Marin (1883–1969)
Recipes: loose pages of recipes written in code, with legends on first page, held in card folder
22 × 14 cm
The British Museum Department of Ethnography Library

Gaspard Marin (1883–1969)
Two hardback notebooks containing stamps and notes collected during his travels (in Europe and the Far East respectively)
21 × 14 cm
The British Museum Department of Ethnography Library

The Metre, 1889
90% / 10% platinum-iridium
102 × 2 × 2 cm
The National Physical Laboratory

Lisa Milroy
Stamps, 1990
oil on canvas
203 × 260 cm
The artist, courtesy Waddington Galleries

'Mines' sign
French military

Model of radium needle
metal, ceramic
44 × 1.8 cm
The National Physical Laboratory

Pedro Moitinho
Nouns, 1998
performance installation – video back-projection, platform, desk, computer, fax machine and 20 metres of fax paper

Mole trap, 19th century
elm, iron, string
Birmingham Museums & Art Gallery

Mortar and pestle, 17th–18th century
boxwood
Birmingham Museums & Art Gallery

Mouse trap, 1700–1850
oak, wood, metal, textile
Birmingham Museums & Art Gallery

Bruce Nauman
AH HA, 1975
screenprint printed on Arches paper
edition of 44 published by Gemini GEL, Los Angeles
74 × 104.5 cm
Private collection

Mariele Neudecker
The Air We Breathe is Invisible, 1992–96
photo album, glue, carved map of Channel between Great Britain and France, glass
12.2 × 36.1 × 45.5 cm
Courtesy of Lotta Hammer Gallery/the artist

L. Noke
Handling a Balloon by Searchlight, WWII
conté and chalk on silk
21.5 × 57.1 cm
Imperial War Museum, London

Pair of crushed car wheels
Richard Freeth Recycling

Simon Patterson
The Great Bear, 1992
colour lithograph on paper
101.6 × 127 cm
Arts Council Collection, Hayward Gallery, London

Charles Pears
A Dazzled Merchantman, WWI
oil on canvas
40.6 × 60.9 cm
Imperial War Museum, London

Charles Pears
A Drifting Mine, 1918
oil on canvas
35.5 × 45.7 cm
Imperial War Museum, London

6 plastic toy farm animals, labelled Bull, Cow, Horse, Mule, Pig, Sheep

John Riddy
Normandy, 1992
photograph
38 × 48 cm
Courtesy of Frith Street Gallery, London

John Riddy
Santiago De Compostela (Radio House), 1998
photograph
38 × 48 cm
Courtesy of Frith Street Gallery, London

Gerrit Thomas Rietveld
First sketch for shop window display, c.1938
pencil, pen and ink on the back of draft of letter to the sculptor Bijerman
23.5 × 29 cm
The Victoria and Albert Museum

Karin Ruggaber
Buffer, 1998
fake leather, foam, timber
9 × 233 × 9.5 cm
Collection of the artist

Karin Ruggaber
Fur Machine, 1998
fake fur, rollers, motor, chipboard
22 × 60 × 40 cm
Collection of the artist

Tom Sachs
Nuke the Swiss, 1996
Self-adhesive sticker, edition of 7,500
each 7.5 × 7.5 cm
Private collection

Set of 7 flat-sided plastic farmyard models overprinted with identifying markings

'Shower' sign
British military

5 simulated bones
red rubber
Private collection

Split tally stick, 1824
wood
67 × 2.5 × 1.5 cm; 60 × 2.5 × 0.5 cm
The Governor and Company of the Bank of England

Stadthaus im Abbruch
Pair of ready to assemble models – town house in process of demolition
Contemporary German

12 standard egg poises
aluminium
10.2 × 30.5 × 15.2 cm, including mount
National Weights and Measures Laboratory

Studio of Walt Disney
Preliminary sketch of Pluto the Dog, for animated film The Dog Show, 1936
pencil on paper
25.5 × 30.5 cm
The Victoria and Albert Museum

Teetotum ball (dice)
mahogany
Birmingham Museums & Art Gallery

This is a Rest Centre, WWII
lithograph on paper
50.6 × 76.3 cm
Imperial War Museum, London

Toushi-Radar Chart Book, 1998

Percyval Tudor-Hart
Square sample of linen painted with camouflaged pattern; unfinished irregular-shaped part of camouflaged sniper suit (possibly the hood), 1917
matt oil-based paints on linen
45 × 45 cm; 66 × 48 cm
Imperial War Museum, London

10 tulip bulbs: single white, 'Diana'

Tyre mould
steel back with aluminium
approximately 76.2 × 76.2 × 17.8 cm
Goodyear Great Britain Limited

Unit of Thought
2 laser-scanned confocal microscopic images of a part of a cultured nerve cell from a mouse hippocampus
25 × 20 cm
Courtesy of Dr Tim Bliss

Sir John Vanbrugh
Castle Howard, c.1700
pen and ink on paper
36.5 × 26.5 cm
The Victoria and Albert Museum

War Office
Map of Europe, WWII
silk
55 × 55 cm
Imperial War Museum, London

Alison Wilding
Infinities – 1, 1991
bronze meteorite cast in resin
Collection William Louis-Dreyfus

Wimbel (stook binder), 19th century
pine, iron
Birmingham Museums & Art Gallery

Bill Woodrow
Our World, 1997
cast bronze
5 × 3.5 cm
The British Art Medal Society

Bill Woodrow
Mould for Our World
silicone rubber mould
7.7 × 8.5 × 2.5 cm
Nicola Moss

Bill Woodrow
Wax model for Our World
wax floating in water in jam jar
jar is 8 × 6.5 cm split in half
Nicola Moss

Elizabeth Wright
BSA Tour Of Britain Racer Enlarged to 135%, 1996/97
steel, rubber and plastic
124 × 236 × 55 cm
The Saatchi Gallery, London

The Yard, copy, c.1845
iron, brass
96 × 4 × 4.5 cm
The National Physical Laboratory

Kumi Yokoyu
A woman was born into the world – 1914, 1998
chrome print and laser print
90 × 105 cm; 102 × 56.2 cm
Courtesy of the artist

Young child's fashion flak jacket
printed cotton with padding
Private collection